Return to the City

of

White Donkeys

ALSO BY JAMES TATE

The Lost Pilot

The Oblivion Ha-Ha

Hints to Pilgrims

Absences

Viper Jazz

Riven Doggeries

Constant Defender

Reckoner

Distance from Loved Ones

Selected Poems

Worshipful Company of Fletchers

Shroud of the Gnome

Memoir of the Hawk

PROSE

The Route as Briefed

Dreams of a Robot Dancing Bee

Return to the City

of

White Donkeys

poems

JAMES TATE

ecco
An Imprint of HarperCollinsPublishers

HarperCollins books may be purchased for educational, business, or sales promotional use. For information, please e-mail the Special Markets Department at SPsales@harpercollins.com.

FIRST ECCO PAPERBACK EDITION 2005

Designed by Cassandra J. Pappas

The Library of Congress has catalogued the hardcover edition as follows:

Tate, James, 1943–
    Return to the city of white donkeys : poems / James Tate.—1st ed.
        p.   cm.
      ISBN 0-06-075001-4
      1. Prose poems, American. I. Title.
    PS3570.A8R47 2004
    811'.54—dc22

                                                          2004046948

ISBN-10: 0-06-075002-2 (pbk.)
ISBN-13: 978-0-06-075002-2

                    15   BVG/❖   10   9   8   7   6

For Dara

Acknowledgments

Agni, American Poetry Review, Bellevue Literary Review, Both, Boston Review, canwehaveourballback, Conjunctions, Crab Orchard Review, Crowd, Cue, Fence, Field, The Germ, The Gettysburg Review, Harvard Review, Hunger Mountain, jubilat, The Massachusetts Review, New Letters, The New Yorker. New American Writing, Pleiades, Poetry, Prairie Schooner, Raritan, Quick Fictions, The Three Penny Review, Tin House, TriQuarterly, Virginia Quarterly Review, Washington Square, The Yale Review.

I would also like to thank the Poetry Center of Chicago for printing a broadside of "Shiloh," and Sarabande Books for a selection of these poems, LOST RIVER, in their Quarternote Chapbook Series.

Contents

Long-Term Memory   1

The Memories of Fish   2

The Beautiful Shoeshine   3

Never Enough Darts   4

It Happens Like This   5

Brittle Family Photographs   6

The Man Without Leather Breeches   7

The All but Perfect Evening on the Lake   8

The Florist   10

Lost River   11

Making the Best of the Holidays   13

Their Number Became Thinned   14

Lust for Life   15

The Incense Man   17

The Lost Chapter   18

Bernie at the Pay Phone   20

Suburban Bison   21

In Search Of   22

Banking Rules   23

The Animists   24

The Healing Ground   25

The Promotion   27

A Sound Like Distant Thunder   28

A Cyclops Would Have Been Better   29

Of Whom Am I Afraid?   30

The Camel   31

Condolence   32

Silver Queen   33

The Ravine   34

The Bleeding Mind   36

Etiquette   37

The Greater Battle   38

The Fragrant Cloud   40

Hunger   41

Sheldon's Derring-Do   42

Half-Eaten   44

Jules to the Rescue   45

The Found Penny   46

Holy Saturday   47

The Formal Invitation   49

A More Prosperous Nation   51

Mr. Twiggy   53

Intruders   55

Bounden Duty   56

Seven Sauce Lobster of Paradise   58

Shiloh   60

The Interview   61

In a Past Life   62

Not Long Ago, Milk Cows Ruminated There   63

Beavertown   64

Love Child   65

Sleepy Visitation   66

Elysium   68

Why We Must Sleep   70

I Never Meant to Harm Him   72

A Trout in the Tam o' Shanter   74

Swoon   76

The Historical Society   77

The Wild Turkey   79

Directions to the Peace Pagoda   80

The Rules   82

Wendell   84

The Survivalists   86

The Rally   88

The Case of Aaron Novak   90

The Rebel   92

The Harp   94

Kung Fu Dancing   96

Special Protection   98

The Cobbler's Assistant   100

The Special Guest   102

Faultfinding Tour   104

The Loon   106

The New Mountain   107

Red Dirt   109

Lost Geese   110

The Long Journey Home   112

Kingdom Come   114

Conventional Medicine   116

How the People Live   118

The Aphid Farmers   120

The Visiting Scholar   122

The Reenactors   124

The Boy Band   126

Things Change   128

The Sinking Boat   130

The Radish   132

Affliction   134

Bringing in the New Year   136

The Petition   137

Trail of Miracles   139

The Prehensile Tail   141

The Reluctant Surrender of an Important Piece of Evidence   143

Song of the Nightingales   145

Return to the City of White Donkeys   147

The Raven Speaks   149

The Great Horned Owl Has Flown   151

The Nameless Ones   153

The Bus Stop   155

Voyage to an Outlying Island   157

Macaroni   159

The Coolest Thing   161

A Clean Hit   163

The Kennedy Assassination   165

The Investors   167

The Vacant Jungle   169

A Sunday Drive   171

Being Present at More Than One Place at a Time   172

The Search for Lost Lives   173

"The trees reflected in the river—they are unconscious of a spiritual world so near them. So are we."

—Nathaniel Hawthorne,
The American Notebooks

Return to the City
of
White Donkeys

Long-Term Memory

I was sitting in the park feeding pigeons
when a man came over to me and scrutinized my
face right up close. "There's a statue of you
over there," he said. "You should be dead. What
did you do to deserve a statue?" "I've never seen
a statue of me," I said. "There can't be a statue
of me. I've never done anything to deserve a
statue. And I'm definitely not dead." "Well,
go look for yourself. It's you alright, there's
no mistaking that," he said. I got up and walked
over where it was. It was me alright. I looked
like I was gazing off into the distance, or the
future, like those statues of pioneers. It didn't
have my name on it or anything, but it was me.
A lady came up to me and said, "You're looking at
your own statue. Isn't that against the law, or
something?" "It should be," I said, "but this is
my first offense. Maybe they'll let me off light."
"It's against nature, too," she said, "and bad
manners, I think." "I couldn't agree with you
more," I said. "I'm walking away right now, sorry."
I went back to my bench. The man was sitting there.
"Maybe you're a war hero. Maybe you died in the
war," he said. "Never been a soldier," I said.
"Maybe you founded this town three hundred years
ago," he said. "Well, if I did, I don't remember
it now," I said. "That's a long time ago," he
said, "you coulda forgot." I went back to feeding
the pigeons. Oh, yes, founding the town. It was
coming back to me now. It was on a Wednesday.
A light rain, my horse slowed . . .

The Memories of Fish

Stanley took a day off from the office
and spent the whole day talking to fish in
his aquarium. To the little catfish scuttling
along the bottom he said, "Vacuum that scum,
boy. Suck it up, that's your job." The skinny
pencil fish swam by and he said, "Scribble,
scribble, scribble. Write me a novel, needle-
nose." The angel executed a particularly
masterful left turn and Stanley said, "You're
no angel, but you sure can drive." Then he broke
for lunch and made himself a tuna fish sandwich,
the irony of which did not escape him. Oh no,
he wallowed in it, savoring every bite. Then
he returned to his chair in front of the aquarium.
A swarm of tiny neons amused him. "What do you
think this is, Times Square!" he shouted. And
so it went long into the night. The next morning
Stanley was horribly embarrassed by his behavior
and he apologized to the fish several times,
but they never really forgave him. He had mocked
their very fishiness, and for this there can be
no forgiveness.

The Beautiful Shoeshine

There was no one in the airport. I
couldn't believe it, so I walked down hallway
after hallway. No passengers, no airline
personnel, no one in the little shops and
restaurants. It was spooky. I had a plane
to catch. I had to get to Chicago. But
actually that was a minor detail compared
to the overwhelming sense of otherworldliness
I was experiencing being alone in this huge
terminal, which is always bustling with
hordes of travelers and employees.
Finally, I saw a shoeshine man sitting alone
on his stand. I walked up to him and he
smiled and said, "Shoeshine, Mister?"
"Sure," I said. "You must be having kind of
a slow day," I added. "I'm doing fine," he
said. "It just seems the more people fly
the harder it is to see them." I looked
around. Some blurs were dashing
for the gates, others were asking the time
in high squeaky voices. It must be my fault,
just not flying enough.

Never Enough Darts

A bear walked right into town last week.
It was a big one, too, a male. It pushed open
the door of the pizza place and ate all the
pizza off the customers' plates. People just
sat there with their mouths open, impressed.
Then he just walked on down the street and went
in the hamburger joint and did the same thing.
The cook managed to call the police. The police
came right away, but they had used up all of
their knock out darts at last Friday night's
high school football game. So they just followed
the bear at a polite distance. When the bear
was full it found its way out of town. The
people I talked to seemed delighted to be getting
back to nature. As long as they had enough to
eat they weren't going to complain.

It Happens Like This

I was outside St. Cecilia's Rectory
smoking a cigarette when a goat appeared beside me.
It was mostly black and white, with a little reddish
brown here and there. When I started to walk away,
it followed. I was amused and delighted, but wondered
what the laws were on this kind of thing. There's
a leash law for dogs, but what about goats? People
smiled at me and admired the goat. "It's not my goat,"
I explained. "It's the town's goat. I'm just taking
my turn caring for it." "I didn't know we had a goat,"
one of them said. "I wonder when my turn is." "Soon,"
I said. "Be patient. Your time is coming." The goat
stayed by my side. It stopped when I stopped. It looked
up at me and I stared into its eyes. I felt he knew
everything essential about me. We walked on. A police-
man on his beat looked us over. "That's a mighty
fine goat you got there," he said, stopping to admire.
"It's the town's goat," I said. "His family goes back
three hundred years with us," I said, "from the beginning."
The officer leaned forward to touch him, then stopped
and looked up at me. "Mind if I pat him?" he asked.
"Touching this goat will change your life," I said.
"It's your decision." He thought real hard for a minute,
and then stood up and said, "What's his name?" "He's
called the Prince of Peace," I said. "God! This town
is like a fairy tale. Everywhere you turn there's mystery
and wonder. And I'm just a child playing cops and robbers
forever. Please forgive me if I cry." "We forgive you,
Officer," I said. "And we understand why you, more than
anybody, should never touch the Prince." The goat and
I walked on. It was getting dark and we were beginning
to wonder where we would spend the night.

Brittle Family Photographs

It's hard work and the pay is low, but at
least you get to hang out with a bunch of nasty,
bitter people. So I took the job. The first
week I thought I'd die. I couldn't stop my hands
from bleeding, and my legs could barely hold me
up. The second week my eyes were blurred and I
couldn't keep my food down. By the fourth week
I was beginning to like it. I felt strong. After
a year I felt nothing. I didn't know my name,
I didn't know where I was. Whatever it was I
was supposed to do got done, but I don't know how.
Then I met Deidre in the cafeteria and she said,
"Mr. President, you're doing a great job." "What
did you call me?" I said. "Mr. President," she
said. "How time pisses away," I said. "I can
hear the birdies singing." My eye was on the
Jell-O.

Grocery shopping can be such a mysterious
business. When a complete stranger smiles and
nods hello to me I wonder what it means. Some-
thing like, "We're both still eating. That's
good. And we're gathering more food, both of
us. We have so much in common we might as well
be friends." I look to see what he has in his
basket. It's not at all similar to what I have
in mine. If ever I were to have an enemy it
would be this man, with all his grains and root
vegetables. I begin to follow him at a polite
distance. He turns into the homeopathic medicine
aisle and lingers there a long time. Altogether
he puts eleven vials into his cart. He sees
that I'm watching him and he smiles again, as
though I would understand the wisdom of his
choices. I don't. He looks healthy, maybe
too healthy. "That stuff costs a fortune and
can't cure the sniffles," I want to tell him.
By now I've forgotten what I came for. Everyone
is smiling at me as though I were completely
naked. I look down and I am completely naked.
And that's what I find so mysterious about
grocery shopping, how that could be.

The All but Perfect Evening on the Lake

We were at the lake for the weekend. We
had just come back from canoeing. We had seen
the loons and a couple of deer and an eagle.
Cleo was taking a shower and I had just opened
a bottle of wine. There was a fire going in
the fireplace. I had worked hard for all of
this, but still I felt like the luckiest man
on earth. When Cleo finally joined me I knew
it was true. She was stunning. "It was a great
day, honey," she said, "thank you." "You're
what makes it great for me, and I can't thank
you enough," I said. I poured us some wine and
we stared at the fire. About an hour later,
there was a knock at the door. This in itself
was a little disconcerting because there are so
few people around here. I looked at Cleo and
she shrugged her shoulders and grimaced. I
opened the door and there was a ranger standing
there. "Are you Eric and Cleo Martin?" he asked.
"Yes, sir," I said. "What seems to be the
problem?" "You're under arrest," he said.
"What in the world for?" I asked, utterly
confused. "Too much happiness," he said.
"The folks around here have registered several
complaints, and there are laws that limit this
kind of thing on the lake. You'll both have
to come with me." "Is this some kind of joke?"
I asked. "I'll have to look in my book," he
said. And then he pulled a thick leather
book out of his coat and carefully turned the
pages until he found the appropriate entry.
He studied it for a minute or so, running
his finger down the page. Finally
he said, "Yes, definitely, this is some kind of
joke, but I'm unable to determine which
kind. Is that okay, would that bother you

if I can't tell you what kind of joke it is?"
I looked at Cleo. "We don't care. Well,
goodnight, officer. Have a good evening."
"And you folks go right back to being happy,"
he said. "Goodnight."

The Florist

I realized Mother's Day was just two days
away, so I went into the florist and said, "I'd
like to send my mother a dozen long-stem red
roses." The guy looked at me and said, "My mother's
dead." I thought this was slightly unprofessional
of him, so I said, "How much would that be?" He
wiped his eyes and said, "Oh, that's all right. I'm
over it, really. She never loved me anyway, so why
should I grieve." "Can they be delivered by Thursday?"
I inquired. "She hated flowers," he said. "I've
never known a woman to hate flowers the way she did.
She wanted me to be a dentist, like her father.
Can you imagine that, torturing people all day.
Instead, I give them pleasure. She disowned me,
really. And yet I miss her," and then he started
crying again. I gave him my handkerchief and he
blew his nose heartily into it. My annoyance had
given way to genuine pity. This guy was a mess.
I didn't know what to do. Finally I said, "Listen,
why don't you send a dozen roses to my mother. You
can tell her you are a friend of mine. My mother
loves flowers, and she'll love you for sending them
to her." He stopped crying and scowled at me. "Is
this some kind of trick? A trap or something, to
get me tied up in a whole other mother thing, because
if it is, I mean, I just got rid of one, and I can't
take it, another I mean, I'm not as strong as I
appear. . . ." "Forget it," I said, "it was a bad idea,
and I'm certainly not sending my mother any flowers
this year, that, too, was a bad idea. Will you be
all right if I leave now, I have other errands, but
if you need me I can stay." "Yes, if you could stay
with me awhile. My name is Skeeter and Mother's
Day is always such a trial for me. I miss her more
every passing day," he said. And so we sat there
holding hands for an hour or so, and then I was on
my way to the cleaners, the bank and the gas station.

Lost River

Jill and I had been driving for hours
on these little back country roads and we hadn't
seen another car or a store of any kind in all
that time. We were trying to get to a village
called Lost River and we were running out of gas.
There was a man there that owns a pterodactyl
wing and we heard that he might want to sell it.
He was tired of it, we were told. Finally, I see
an old pickup truck coming up behind us and I
pull over and get out of the car and wave. The
man starts to pass us by, but changes his mind
and stops. I ask him if he knows how to get to Lost
River and he says he's never heard of it, but
can give us directions to the closest town called
Last Grocery Store. I thank him and we eventually
find Last Grocery Store, which consists of three
trailers and a little bitsy grocery store. The
owner is old and nearly blind, but he's glad to
meet us and we're glad to meet him. I ask him
if he knows how to get to Lost River from here.
He ponders for a while, and then says, "I don't
see how you could get there, unless you're walking.
There's no road out in them parts. Why would
anybody be wanting to go to Lost River, there's
nothing there." "There's a man there that's got
a pterodactyl wing he might be willing to sell,"
I say. "Hell, I'll sell you mine. I can't see
it anymore, so I might as well sell it," he says.
Jill and I look at each other, incredulous. "Well,
we'd sure like to see it," I say. "No problem,"
he says, "I keep it right here in back of the store."
He brings it out and it's beautiful, delicate
and it's real, I'm certain of it. The foot even
has its claws on it. We're speechless and rather
terrified of holding it, though he hands it to us
trustingly. My whole body feels like it's vibrating,
like I'm a harp of time. I'm sort of embarrassed,

but finally I ask him how much he wants for it.
"Oh, just take it. It always brought me luck, but
I've had all the luck I need," he says. Jill gives
him a kiss on the cheek and I shake his hand and
thank him. Tomorrow: Lost River.

Justine called on Christmas day to say she
was thinking of killing herself. I said, "We're
in the middle of opening presents, Justine. Could
you possibly call back later, that is, if you're
still alive." She was furious with me and called
me all sorts of names which I refuse to dignify
by repeating them. I hung up on her and returned
to the joyful task of opening presents. Everyone
seemed delighted with what they got, and that
definitely included me. I placed a few more logs
on the fire, and then the phone rang again. This
time it was Hugh and he had just taken all of his
pills and washed them down with a quart of gin.
"Sleep it off, Hugh," I said, "I can barely under-
stand you, you're slurring so badly. Call me
tomorrow, Hugh, and Merry Christmas." The roast
in the oven smelled delicious. The kids were playing
with their new toys. Loni was giving me a big
Christmas kiss when the phone rang again. It was
Debbie. "I hate you," she said. "You're the most
disgusting human being on the planet." "You're
absolutely right," I said, "and I've always been
aware of this. Nonetheless, Merry Christmas, Debbie."
Halfway through dinner the phone rang again, but
this time Loni answered it. When she came back
to the table she looked pale. "Who was it?" I
asked. "It was my mother," she said. "And what
did she say?" I asked. "She said she wasn't my
mother," she said.

Judd wrecked his car driving home from
my place the other night. He hit a patch of
black ice and the car spun around out of control
and crashed into a tree. Luckily he wasn't hurt,
and the police report didn't charge him with
anything. When he was telling me about it the
next morning, he went silent for a moment, and
then he said, "I think I hit three little children."
I was shocked because Judd is, for the most part,
a really sane man. "But, Judd," I said, "the
police were there, they filed a report. Trust me,
you didn't hit anyone." "When the car was spinning,"
he said, "I caught the flash of their faces in
the headlights. There was terror in their eyes.
They looked right at me. I saw them, honest, I
did." "I guess this kind of thing is understand-
able," I said, "given the panic and fear you felt,
but, really, Judd, you didn't hit any children."
I attributed this irrational state of mind to
shock, and assumed it would pass quickly. But
it didn't. In a matter of weeks he began referring
to the kids by name—Tess, Marla and Cliff. And
I stopped protesting. It's just that he was so
convincing. He would tell me episodes from their
lives. He never mentioned their families. It
was as though they were waifs, playing their
innocent games, biding their time, and always
waiting for Judd's car to hit that black ice.
Eventually, Judd had photographs of them framed,
and when I saw them I recognized them at once.

Veronica has the best apartment in town.
It's on the third story and has big plate glass
windows that look straight down on the town common.
She has a bird's-eye view of all the protesters,
the fairs, the lovers, people eating lunch on
park benches; in general, the life blood of the
town. The more Veronica watched all these little
dramas, the less desire she had to actually go
out and be one herself. I called her from time
to time, but her conversation consisted of her
descriptions of what was going on in the common.
"Now he's kissing her and saying good-bye. He's
getting on the bus. The bus is pulling out.
Wait a minute, she's just joined hands with
another guy. I can't believe it! These people
are behaving like trash. There's a real tiny
old lady with a walker trying to go into the
bookstore, but she keeps stopping and looking
over her shoulder. She thinks she's being
followed." "Veronica," I say, "I'm dying."
"Two of the richest and nastiest lawyers in
town are arguing over by the drinking fountain.
They're actually shouting, I can almost hear
them. Oh my god, one of them has shoved the
other. It's incredible, Artie. You should be
here," she says. "War has been declared with
England, Veronica. Have you heard that?" I
say. "That's great, Artie," she says. "Remember
the girl who kissed the guy getting on the bus
and then immediately took up with the other guy?
Well, now she's flirting with the parking officer
and he's loving it and flirting back with her.
He just tore up a ticket he had written for her.
I'm really beginning to like this girl after all."
"That's great, Veronica," I say. "Why don't

you check and see if your little panties are
on fire yet," and I hang up, and I don't think
she even notices. I wonder if I'm supposed to
be worried about her. But in the end I don't.
Veronica has the best apartment in town.

The Incense Man

Outside the Cigar Store a man was selling
incense. "It's very romantic," he said to me.
"I can't stand that stuff," I said. "Women love
it," he said. "It makes them want to make love."
"Not the women I know. That stuff would make
them leave me high and dry in a second," I said.
"You don't know the right women then. I could
introduce you to some. They all love this stuff,"
he said. This guy was really getting on my nerves.
"What are you, some kind of pimp? You stand
around the street selling this vile crap, and
then trying to sell women as well," I said.
"I didn't say anything about selling women. I
just said I could introduce you to some, some
real women who like to make love while smelling
this beautiful incense. That's no crime, I was
trying to be friendly and look where you take it,
calling me a pimp. If I weren't such a peace-
loving guy, I'd bust your ass," he said. Across
the street an old man on crutches fell down. "How
much is it?" I asked. People were helping the
old man up. His best days were over, that's for
sure. But he seemed determined to get somewhere.
"For you, they're a hundred dollars a stick," he
said. "Come on," I said, "I'm sorry I said what
I said. Let's forgive and forget. I'd really
like to buy some of that stuff," I said. "How
do you think it makes me feel selling this stuff,
huh? I'm a grown man and I'm selling incense on
the street. Is that a pretty picture? Do you
want to walk in my shoes?" he said. "Sorry, man,"
I said, and walked away. A flock of pigeons
perched atop the First National Bank suddenly
took flight, and I thought, this day is not over
yet.

I was sitting in the coffee shop reading
the paper when Tracy walked in looking like
she slept in a haystack after drinking, well,
a lot. She saw me and came over and sat down.
"Jesus," I said, "what happened to you?" "You're
not going to believe it," she said. "I was
home alone last night and I had this bottle of
bourbon and for no good reason I decided to fix
myself a drink. I mean, I'm not really a drinker
but for some reason last night it seemed like
a good idea. Well, I poured myself a good one
and halfway through the drink everything started
to seem so funny. I had the radio on and all
the songs made me laugh out loud. Anyway, I
was having such a good time all by myself and
before I knew it, I had drunk the whole damned bottle.
I was royally shit-faced. "So what happened?"
I asked, because she was looking off in space.
"That's the trouble, I don't really know. I
woke up this morning in a haystack somewhere
next to this guy named Keith. He's an electrician."
"Keith Hamilton," I said. "I know him a little
bit." "Yeah, Keith Hamilton. That's him,"
she said. "And I don't know what happened.
I'm so ashamed of myself." "Maybe nothing
happened," I said. "I mean, nothing you'd have
to be ashamed about. But you do have a lot of
straw in your hair, which is rather fetching."
"What should I do?" she said. "Well, I guess
joining the Witness Protection Program is out
since you didn't actually witness anything,"
I joked. "I've always felt pretty romantic
about haystacks and barns." "But what if I
was an animal?" she said. "An animal in a
barn is natural enough, and I doubt if they
remember much about the night before," I said,
trying to help. "What if I slept with a goat?"

she asked. The people at two separate tables
jerked their heads around and glared at Tracy
with her hair full of straw. "Lucky goat,"
I said. We both smiled politely at the
eavesdroppers.

Bernie at the Pay Phone

I came out of the post office and there
was Bernie Stapleton talking on a pay phone.
Bernie had been hiding from me for seven years.
I had loaned him a thousand dollars for an emer-
gency and I never heard from him again. He wasn't
sure if I had recognized him, so he turned his
back to me and hung his head down. Bernie didn't
know what it was to earn a living. He just moved
from one scam to another, narrowly evading the
law. But I had always had a soft spot in my
heart for Bernie. I waited at a certain distance
for him to get off the phone. I knew he was
sweating blood. "Bernie," I said, "where have
you been? I've missed you." He was massively
uncomfortable. "I've been away. I've been running
an investment firm in the Bahamas. Yeah, I've
missed you, too. How've you been?" "Well, to
tell you the truth, I'm kind of down on my luck,"
I said, which was a lie. "Maybe I could help
you out, Simon. If you could come up with, say,
a couple hundred bucks, I could turn it into
something substantial real fast," he said.
Bernie never changed. Everything around us was
changing so fast I couldn't keep up, and there was
Bernie at the pay phone making nickel and dime
deals the way he's always done. "I think I
could come up with that much," I said. "Then
meet me here tomorrow at three. A little favor
for an old friend, that's the least I can do."
Bernie was standing tall now. He really believed
he was an investment banker in the Bahamas,
and not some scuzzy little rat holed up in
Shutesbury without a pot to piss in. I admired
that to no end. "Thanks, Bernie, I'll see you
tomorrow," I said.

Suburban Bison

Joshua and I had decided to go bowling.
Neither of us had bowled in years, and we didn't
really like to bowl, so it made no sense. We
were driving down Route 9 when we spotted the
buffalo herd. They were grazing in the snow,
and something about their improbable heads made
me catch my breath. I pulled over to the side
of the road. "Why are they here?" Joshua asked.
"I guess it's some kind of cruel joke," I said.
"Well, it's not funny," he said. "They're way
too majestic. Buffalo are supposed to roam,
that's what the song says, not be penned up
along some strip for tourists to see," he
said. "It beats bowling," I said. And so we
sat there for the next hour contemplating the
life of the postmodern buffalo, deconstructing
their owners, and never putting them back
together again.

Angela was sleeping all the time now, except
for some quick meals and the odd bath. When we
ate together she could barely talk. Finally I
felt I had to say something. "Angela," I said,
"I don't think this is good for you. You need
exercise. And your mind—" "I'm looking for
something," she said, "something that will change
our lives. And I'm getting closer. I think I may
find it within a week. Please, trust me, be
patient with me," she said. "What is it, Angela?
What is it you are looking for?" I said. "I can't
tell you. It would bring bad luck. You'll just
have to trust me," she said, and went back to bed.
During the following week we barely spoke. Then
the next day she jumped out of bed, showered,
dressed and declared she was starving. She made
herself an enormous meal and gulped it all down
breathlessly. "Well, did you find it?" I asked.
"Yeah, but it was a fake," she said. "What did
you think it was going to be?" I asked. "I thought
it was a finger of Saint John the Dwarf buried
beneath the tulip tree out back, put there by
marauding Berbers fifteen hundred years ago.
But it turns out it's just a plastic spoon," she
said. I paused to let it all sink in. "Just
think," I said, "a little piece of John the Dwarf
in our backyard. And those marauding Berbers.
I can see why you were excited."

Banking Rules

I was standing in line at the bank and
the fellow in front of me was humming. The
line was long and slow, and after a while
the humming began to irritate me. I said to
the fellow, "Excuse me, would you mind not
humming." And he said, "Was I humming?
I'm sorry, I didn't realize it." And he went
right on humming. I said, "Sir, you're
humming again." "Me, humming?" he said.
"I don't think so." And then he went on
humming. I was about to blow my lid. Instead,
I went to find the manager. I said, "See
that man over there in the blue suit?" "Yes,"
he said, "what about him?" "He won't stop
humming," I said, "I've asked him politely
several times, but he won't stop." "There's
no crime in humming," he said. I went back
and took my place in line. I listened, but
there was nothing coming out of him. I said,
"Are you okay, pal?" He looked mildly peeved,
and gave me no reply. I felt myself shrinking.
The manager of the bank walked briskly up
to me and said, "Sir, are you aware of the
fact that you're shrinking?" I said I was.
And he said, "I'm afraid we don't allow that
kind of behavior in this bank. I have to ask
you to leave." The air was whistling out
of me, I was almost gone.

The Animists

At the motel, the man said, "This is a
Christian motel. I've got to see your marriage
license." "Marriage license?" I said. "We don't
drive around with our marriage license. I don't
even know where it is, but it sure isn't in the
car." "Then you can't stay here. We don't allow
heathens," he said. "Heathens?" I said. "You're
calling us heathens?" "The world's full of them,"
he said. "Whether you're among them, I don't know.
But I don't take chances." "And how do we know
you're not some kind of child molester or ax
murderer," Melissa said. I was proud of her.
"Show him your tits," I said. Melissa lifted up
her sweater and showed him her God-given natural
endowment. The old man gawked and stammered, "You . . .
you . . . appear to be Christian." "Nope," she said,
"the left one's an animist and the right one is
too private to even discuss religion, but my guess
is that she's an animist, too." "I like animists,"
he said, "I love animists. They're my favorite."
We turned and headed for the door. "Dirty old
man," I said. "You're right," he said. "I am
a dirty old Christian man. I didn't know that.
Thank you and come back any time."

The Healing Ground

Mimi was going to take me to her special
place, some kind of sacred healing ground, though
she never said whose. For over a year walking had
caused me great pain, and none of the doctors I
had seen gave me any help. I viewed Mimi's invitation
as an excuse for an outing. I know the country
around here pretty well, but when Mimi started
turning down one twisting dirt road after another
at some point I knew I was lost. Mimi's a reliable
person, nothing of the fruitcake in her. When she
finally stopped, the first thing I noticed was a
hole in the side of the hill surrounded by boulders.
"What's that?" I said. "An Irish monk lived in there
some time in the sixteenth century," she said.
"The Indians took care of him. They thought he
was a holy man." "Do I have to crawl in there?"
I asked. "Oh no, nothing like that," she said.
"They say he lived in that hole for thirty years,
praying all the time." "I wonder what happened
to him. Did the Church make him a saint?" I said.
"Something ate him, a bear or a mountain lion. The
Indians thought it was a mountain lion," she said.
"Mimi," I said, "did you bring me all the way out
here just to tell me this story, not that it isn't
a great story, 'cause it is, but I'd also love to
see this 'healing ground,' is that possible?"
"It's right over there in that clearing. Come
on, I'll show you," she said. We had to push our
way through the brush and climb over some fallen
trees. It wasn't that easy for me to get there,
but we got there, and I looked around, but could
see nothing special about the place. I mentioned
that to Mimi. "Except for that fairy ring of
mushrooms. That's pretty cute," I said. "You have
to stand in there and pray for the soul of the Irish
monk for ten minutes. That's all," she said. There's
a new fruitcake status in store for you, Mimi, I

thought. "If that's what it takes," I said, "I'll
do it." I proceeded to stand in the circle of
mushrooms with my eyes closed and, sure enough,
I prayed for the soul of the little Irish monk.
He would have had to be little, because the hole
wasn't all that big. I thought of his rosary and
his Bible, and the long winters of terrible cold
and snow. And his great peace when he met the lion.

The Promotion

I was a dog in my former life, a very good
dog, and, thus, I was promoted to a human being.
I liked being a dog. I worked for a poor farmer
guarding and herding his sheep. Wolves and coyotes
tried to get past me almost every night, and not
once did I lose a sheep. The farmer rewarded me
with good food, food from his table. He may have
been poor, but he ate well. And his children
played with me, when they weren't in school or
working in the field. I had all the love any dog
could hope for. When I got old, they got a new
dog, and I trained him in the tricks of the trade.
He quickly learned, and the farmer brought me into
the house to live with them. I brought the farmer
his slippers in the morning, as he was getting
old, too. I was dying slowly, a little bit at a
time. The farmer knew this and would bring the
new dog in to visit me from time to time. The
new dog would entertain me with his flips and
flops and nuzzles. And then one morning I just
didn't get up. They gave me a fine burial down
by the stream under a shade tree. That was the
end of my being a dog. Sometimes I miss it so
I sit by the window and cry. I live in a high-rise
that looks out at a bunch of other high-rises.
At my job I work in a cubicle and barely speak
to anyone all day. This is my reward for being
a good dog. The human wolves don't even see me.
They fear me not.

A Sound Like Distant Thunder

I had fallen asleep on the couch with the
TV on. Every now and then I would open an eye
and see someone get stabbed or eaten by a monster.
Once, a beautiful woman was taking off her blouse.
And then the phone rang. I couldn't tell if it
was a TV phone or my own. I sat up, half-asleep,
and reached for the phone. "Howie," a woman's
voice said, "Is that you? You sound like you were
asleep." "I was," I said. I wasn't Howie, but
I was in the mood to talk to this woman. "Howie,
I miss you. I wish I were in bed with you right
now," she said. "I miss you, too. I wish you
were here with me right now," I said. I hated
not knowing her name, and I didn't know if I could
call her "honey" or "sweetie" or any other endear-
ment. "Why don't you come over right now," I
said. "Oh you know I'm in Australia. And my
work here won't be done for another month. It's
just hell being away from you this long," she said.
"I love you," I said, and I think I meant it.
"You mean the world to me, Howie. I couldn't get
through this without knowing you love me. I think
of you all the time. I look at your picture
every chance I get. It's what gives me strength,
that and our brief phone calls. Now go back to
sleep and dream of me, dream of me kissing you
and holding you. I have to go now. I love you,
Howie," she said and hung up. And though my state
may be described as a gladdened stupor, I felt
like a Howie, I really did, and I believed in my
heart that the nameless, faceless one indentured
in Australia really loved me, and that my great
love for her gave her strength. I cozied up on
the couch and fell into a sweet sleep. But then
I heard a lion roar, and I feared for both of our
lives. "Howie!" she cried. "Save me!" But I
couldn't. I was busy elsewhere, tying my shoe.

A Cyclops Would Have Been Better

The child's left eyelid wouldn't open,
so we captured some urine from an old goat
and froze it into a small cube. Then we held
the cube on the eyelid for twenty-three minutes
and sure enough it was cured. Shortly after
that, the goat died, but we see no connection,
it seemed to be natural causes. The child
always was strange and nothing could change
that. We tried sending him to military school,
but that was a mistake. The last thing he
needed was more strategies for winning wars.
And besides that he was kicked out for firing
his rifle almost constantly. We even hired
a lion tamer and, while he did teach him to
leap through a hoop of fire, the tamer quit
after two weeks, suffering badly from a number
of scratches. We brought in a swami and he
observed Stanley, our son, for several days
before declaring Stanley the Messiah. We
started looking at Stanley in a new way, and
the sad part is, we agree that he may just
be the Messiah, but we don't like him.

Of Whom Am I Afraid?

I was feeling a little at loose ends, so
I went to the Farmer's Supply store and just
strolled up and down the aisles, examining
the merchandise, none of which was of any use
to me, but the feed sacks and seeds had a calm-
ing effect on me. At some point there was an
old, grizzled farmer standing next to me holding
a rake, and I said to him, "Have you ever read
much Emily Dickinson?" "Sure," he said, "I
reckon I've read all of her poems at least a
dozen times. She's a real pistol. And I've
even gotten into several fights about them
with some of my neighbors. One guy said she
was too 'prissy' for him. And I said, 'Hell,
she's tougher than you'll ever be.' When I
finished with him, I made him sit down and read
The Complete Poems over again, all 1,775 of them.
He finally said, 'You're right, Clyde, she's
tougher than I'll ever be.' And he was crying
like a baby when he said that." Clyde slapped
my cheek and headed toward the counter with
his new rake. I bought some ice tongs, which
made me surprisingly happy, and for which I
had no earthly use.

The Camel

I received the strangest thing in the mail
today. It's a photograph of me riding a camel
in the desert. And yet I have never ridden a
camel, or even been in a desert. I am wearing
a jellaba and a keffiyeh and I'm waving a rifle.
I have examined the photo with a magnifying
glass and it is definitely me. I can't stop
looking at the photo. I have never even dreamed
of riding a camel in the desert. The ferocity
in my eyes suggests I am fighting some kind of
holy war, that I have no fear of death. I must
hide this photo from my wife and children. They
must not know who I really am. I must not know.

Condolence

Roddy sat on his couch and sipped his drink
as if a pensive bird lived in his mouth. In between
sips there was silence and a few words, which seemed
enormous. I asked him if he intended to continue
living here now that Allegra was gone. He picked up
a porcelain figure of a dog and examined it for cracks.
"This is not a life," he said. "This is an imitation
of life." "But will you live it here," I said. "Here?
I don't know here from there, or there," he said. "You
have friends here," I said, "people who really care about
you." "People care about their lawns, their cars, their
paychecks. I'm just a charity case," he said. "You're
being cynical, Roddy," I said, "which is understandable
right now, but you have to try and stop it. People
care about you." "I'll tell you the truth, Kris. When
Allegra lay dying in the hospital, in her last hour of
life on this earth, you know what I was thinking about?
I was worried about getting a parking ticket, a fucking
five dollar parking ticket. Can you believe that?"
I picked up the porcelain dog and examined it. "So,
did you get a ticket?" I asked. "I went out to put a
quarter in the meter, and when I came back she had died.
That's how it ended, so you can see why I don't trust
anybody," he said. He sipped at his drink and stared
into space, or what I thought was space. "Roddy," I
said, "Allegra loved you for just who you are." "But
she didn't know me," he said. "She knew," I said.
"She told me everything. She called me when you left
the room. Her last words were, 'I hope he doesn't get
a ticket.' " Roddy smiled for the first time. There
are big lies and then there are little lies. This one seemed
to me to qualify as both. The sun was quickly setting
on this little consolation call. I had a dozen more
to make before the day was over.

Silver Queen

I pulled my car over by the farmstand on
Northwest Street. "How's the corn this year?"
I asked the farmer. "It's the best ever," he
said. "You say that every year," I said. "No
I don't," he said. "Yes you do," I said. "No
I don't," he said. "Yes you do," I said. "I
don't," he said. "Well, you do," I said, "but
let's not make a federal case of it," I said.
"Fair enough," he said. "What kind you got?" I
asked. "Silver Queen," he said. "That's not
Silver Queen," I said. "I know Silver Queen
when I see it and that's not Silver Queen."
"Mister, I've been growing corn for forty-five
years. I know every damned thing there is about
growing corn. I can grow corn in my sleep.
I was growing corn before you were born, and
I'll probably keep right on growing corn after
I die," he said. "If you could stand to part
with a dozen ears of your beautiful Silver Queen,
I'd be much obliged," I said. That night, the
kids all said, "This is the best ever," and
I agreed. The next day I was driving down
Northwest Street again, and I stopped at the
stand and got out and said to the farmer,
"Please forgive me for doubting you. It's
some terrible flaw in me. You were right, it
was the best ever. My children thank you, my
wife thanks you, and I thank you more than
I can ever say," I said. "I forgive you, my
wife forgives you, and the corn forgives you,"
he said, sweeping his arm back toward his fields.
"Oh, yes," I said, "the corn, the corn . . ."

The Ravine

On one side of the country road was a
steep ravine. It was about one hundred and
fifty feet down to a little creek. Cass and I
had been wondering how we could get down there
without breaking our necks. Finally, I said,
"We need a long rope. Tie it to a good tree,
and there you have it." We bought the rope
in town and came back the next day. I went first.
If the knot had slipped, I would have almost
certainly gotten killed. But it didn't, and I
scaled down almost skillfully, considering I
had no experience in this kind of thing. Then
Cass started out. She bumped into a couple of
trees and scraped her ankle on a big rock, but
was laughing all the way down and arrived at
the bottom in one piece. We were excited to
be there, because we knew that practically no
one had ever walked there before. We had
suspected, correctly, that people had been
dumping stuff over the edge of the ravine
for a long time. We found six old washing machines,
an old typewriter, several lamps, hundreds of
rusted-out tin cans, medicine bottles, a kitchen
table, a variety of chairs, a car from the twenties,
nine volumes of the Book of Knowledge, a sombrero,
many shoes and books, a wallet with photos in it.
The list could go on and on. The creek was still
clear and pretty. Cass had brought sandwiches
and we sat on a couple of boulders and ate,
staring into it. "There's a little history
here," Cass said. "I'm not sure what kind,
but, still, something. A museum devoted to
what people no longer want or need." "Imagine
them risen from their graves, standing up there
on the ridge right now, looking down on us

examining their cast-offs. What do you think
they would say?" I said. "I can see them,"
Cass said. "They're all barefooted and they
want their shoes back, but they're too proud to
say anything. They're just staring at us."

A great man was giving a lecture in a town
about thirty miles from here. The lecture was called
"Modern and Contemporary Documented Cases of Stigmata,
or, The Bleeding Mind." Cheryl and I were excited
about going. We managed to make several wrong turns
at poorly marked junctures, and arrived at the church
just in time. There were hundreds of cars parked
up and down Main Street, and a line of people
greater than anything we could have imagined. "Who
would have thought this many people would have been
interested in stigmata?" I said. "It's the whole
crucifixion thing," Cheryl said. "You know, people
say they don't want to be crucified, but then they
go around being obsessed with it. Look at this line,
they all want to know if they're candidates for the
stigmata." "That's crazy," I said, "that's not why
we're here, is it?" "Speak for yourself," she said.
"And, besides, this man, Ian Wilson, is supposed to
be very sexy. He's eighty years old, but with this
long white hair that he whips back and forth as he
speaks. At the end he goes out into the audience
actually weeping as he touches the two or three
people he believes may become stigmatic in their
lifetimes." "Cheryl," I said, "I don't think we're
going to get in. It's a very long line. And, besides,
the looks on some of these peoples' faces are beginning
to scare me." "My god, Aaron, I don't know what you
thought we were going to, a lecture on flatboats of
the Mississippi? This is all or nothing at all. Of
course people are terrified out of their minds,"
she said. "Flatboats of the Mississippi sounds
good to me," I said.

Etiquette

"It sounds like there's someone in the
attic," I said to Gladys. "I'll get my rifle
and check it out." "Oh, Melvin, there's nobody
in the attic. There never is anybody in the
attic." "Oh yeah, what about last time, Miss
Nobody-in-the-Attic." "That was different, Melvin.
You didn't have to be so rough with Mr. Lamkin."
Melvin got his rifle and climbed the rickety
steps to the attic. Gladys heard him yelling
and cursing, and then heard three blasts from
his rifle. When he climbed down a minute later,
she said, "Did you kill him?" "It was that
damned Mr. Lamkin again," he said. "Did you
kill him?" she repeated. "I think he got away,"
Melvin said. "How in the hell did he get away?
There's no windows up there," she said. "I don't
know, Gladys, I just don't know. But I think
he has a nest up there. I'll get him, you just
wait and see, I'll get him," he said. "A nest?"
Gladys said. "Gee, that sounds kind of sweet.
Maybe we could invite him to dinner sometime."

The aquarium in Springfield had opened up
about three years ago, but somehow we just never
found the right time to go. Then one Saturday,
without having planned it, we just jumped in the
car and went. From the moment we entered I felt
the strong magic of the place. One tank would
contain the ghastliest, most hideous fish I had
ever seen in my life, covered with long spikes,
and of course, even they had their otherworldly
beauty. And the next tank would be full of the
most brightly colored, electronically lit-up fish
you could ever imagine. And there were giant
eels, seventy-five feet of churning, black ribbon.
Lauren predicted nightmares, but very sexy ones.
Even the jellyfish were beautiful, their deadly
tentacles, so long and fine, almost like a mane
of hair. From aquarium to aquarium we walked,
holding hands, in a proper state of awe. A
sixteen-foot great white shark had a very long
tank all to himself. He swam restlessly from one
end to the other and back again over and over.
The note on the wall said great whites would attack
boats, that they would eat anything, including
other sharks. We stood there in a small crowd
rapt in fascination. Then, it's hard to explain
what happened next. The shark stopped and seemed
to look straight at me. And the next thing I
knew it was ramming the side of the tank with
all of the power of its enraged tonnage, over
and over again, and the crowd was screaming, and
an attendant came running, and grabbed me by the
arm, and said, "I'm sorry, sir, but I'll have to
ask you to leave. Please, hurry." She led me
out into the courtyard, and Lauren was chasing
after us. "This has never happened before, sir,"
she said. "That shark seems to know you. It
seems to harbor some feelings for you, and I

think it would be best for all if you'd just
leave. The aquarium would insist on refunding
your admission. Please understand." Lauren and
I were speechless, but agreed to leave. On the
way home, we pretended to be amused, but down
deep we were seriously rattled. "Okay, so maybe
I did punch him in the nose once," I said. "What-
ever you say, but he did know you, from somewhere,"
she said.

The Fragrant Cloud

I woke in a spacious room with lavender
wallpaper and brocaded, antique drapes. There
were clothes laid out for me on a fainting
couch. They fit as if they had been tailored
for me. As I descended the staircase, I had
no idea what to expect. A maid showed me to
the breakfast room and brought me coffee and
biscuits. I stared out the window at the gardens.
After a while, a man entered the room and asked
me if I had everything I needed. "Oh yes," I
said, "everything is lovely." "Do you have
any questions?" he asked me. "No," I said.
"Later, Gwen and I will show you around the
grounds," he said. "I look forward to that,"
I said. Then he left me there alone. Gwendolyn.
It's strange how one knows nothing, and, yet,
knows more than one wants to know. I knew that
I would fall in love with Gwendolyn. I knew
that there would be a duel. I knew that this
graceful mansion would burn to the ground. I
sat there waiting, incredibly lonesome with my
awful knowledge.

Hunger

We have a new office manager by the name
of Preston Cooper. I guess he's one of the new
breed, but I like him. He pretends to be very
low-key, when, in fact, his ambition is torqued
to the max. Yesterday, he stuck his head in my
door and said his usual, "How's it going, Mort?"
"I'm talking to Baltimore," I said. "I told them
that, according to my figures, they should double
their units. And, as of this morning, we're lead-
ing the markets in Indianapolis, St. Louis, Chicago
and Kansas City. Bob Bailey just called to tell
me that Tri-Star was pulling out of Minneapolis-
St. Paul altogether." "I smell a big bonus coming
your way, Mortie. Just keep pushing. Don't give
them an inch. Bomb 'em into the Stone Age, as one
of our great leaders used to say," he said, and disappeared
laughing. It's true, since Preston came on board,
it has felt like we've gone to war. We're really
out to kill the other guys. It's fun, but I don't
really know how I feel about it. After all, we're
not talking about protecting our country from the
enemy, we're talking potato chips.

Sheldon called me collect from somewhere
to tell me that I should stay out of the tall
grasses, because the ticks were especially bad
this year. I thanked him for that piece of
information. "Where are you, Sheldon?" I asked.
"I can't tell you," he said. "I'm on a secret
mission, and it wouldn't be a secret if I told
you. I'll tell you all about it soon. Got to
go now. Stay out of the tall grasses." Three
days later he called me again, collect, to remind
me to use strong sunblock if I was going out
into the sun. Then he asked me if I had ever met
Eleanor Roosevelt. "Of course not," I said. "Well,
she's still alive," he said. "They've hidden her
underground in an abandoned mine. She hasn't seen
the light of day in thirty-eight years. I'm going
to rescue her." "Good luck, Sheldon," I said.
"If anyone can do it, you're the man. But be care-
ful." When he didn't call the next week, I was
worried about him. I stayed out of the tall grasses
and wore my sunblock. Then one day I saw Sheldon
sitting outside at the ice-cream parlor. He had
a black eye. "My god," I said, "what happened to
you?" "It's okay," he said, "she's safe. She has
some big plans, too, but I can't tell you about
them now. The world's going to be a better place,
that's all I can tell you . . ." "I'm glad you're
back," I said, "I was really worried about you."
"She wants to meet you," he said. "She has a very
special position for you in her new government.
She's a tough old battle-ax, but you'll love her."
"Eleanor Roosevelt wants to meet me?" I said. "I'd
be honored to serve in her new government." "Soon,
pal, you'll see, the world's going to shine with

her great vision," he said. Sheldon believed every
word he said. And he was right about the ticks.
They were terrible. And a new government headed
by Eleanor Roosevelt sounded great to me. I was
ready to serve.

Half-Eaten

The fortune-teller told me I was going to
come into a large sum of money soon. She told
me my love life would continue to be happy and
satisfying. She said my health would be vigorous.
But then she looked worried. She said there was
some kind of large cat in my near future—a cougar.
And that cat would surprise me when I least expected
it. And that, of course, cancelled out all the
previous good news. I paid her and left her dirty,
little storefront. I looked up and down the street,
checked out the rooftops. Once home, I kissed Jo,
and headed for my study where I looked up Cougar.
Six to eight feet in length, 160 lbs., can drag
five times their weight, can leap twenty feet in
one bound, jump from sixty feet above the ground.
I debated telling Jo. I knew she would ridicule
me. Then I went back in the kitchen and told her.
She stared at me in disgust, incapable of even
finding words at first. Then she said, "You went
to a fortune-teller? And you believe this outrageous
crap about a cougar? And all these years I thought
I was married to a sensible man. What happened
to you, Ralph? Are you on drugs? Have you been
drinking?" "Weirder things have happened," I said.
"Last week a man exploded in Chicago, spontaneous
combustion, walking down the street. There were
witnesses. It was in the paper. There used to be
cougars in these parts, only they called them cata-
mounts or mountain lions. There could be one left,
has a thing for me." "You're not serious, are you,
because, if you are, I'm moving out until your bloody
destiny has reached its climax," she said. It's
strange how alone I felt just then. I thought, it's
just me and the cat, now. I said, "Gee whiz, Jo,
can't you take a little joke. You know I would
never go to a fortune-teller." "Still," she said,
"I can feel it, you're a marked man."

Jules said he would come over and see if
he could fix my stereo. It had not been working
in months, and I had really missed listening to
music. When he arrived, he was all business.
He went right to work. He pulled out all the
wires. "I don't know what you've done here, Mac,
but this is a mess," he said. I just stood back
and watched him. He seemed disgusted, and I
didn't know what to say. "Somebody's tried to
sabotage this whole system," he said. "Do you
have any rye bread?" "I do," I said. "How much
do you need?" "Three slices ought to do it," he
said. I brought them to him and he went on working.
A while later he asked me for a couple of golf balls.
He was working furiously. "How's it going?" I asked.
"We're getting there," he said. "Could you get me
some toothpaste and maybe some pinto beans?" "No
problem," I said. A little scratchy stuff was
beginning to come out of the speakers. Jules was
good. I knew he could help me, if he could find
the time. "One last thing, Mac. Do you think
you could find some Queen Anne's lace in the back-
yard?" "I'll try," I said. I looked and looked
and finally I found just a little bit. "That should
be enough," he said. And he went on working for
another half hour. Then, lo and behold, glorious
music started pouring from the speakers, crisp
and clear as never before. "Thank you, Jules,"
I said, "I thank you from the bottom of my heart."
"Hey, you got to have music. But that's a very
strange system you have there. It's almost human,
it's heading that way. You should keep an eye
on it, and call me if anything funny happens. Okay?"

The Found Penny

Alvin was walking down the street when
he spotted a penny. He stopped to pick it up
and a lady pushing a baby carriage bumped into
him. He tumbled forward and scratched his fore-
head and both elbows. Her baby started cater-
wauling and she barked at Alvin, "Now see what
you have done!" Alvin struggled to his feet.
"But I'm a fiscal conservative. You had no
right to run me down. I'm bleeding real blood.
Your little monster is quite ugly. People always
lie about babies, but I'm telling you the truth,"
he said. She pushed her carriage around Alvin
and harrumphed her way down the street. Alvin
had managed to clutch the penny throughout the
ordeal. A man who had been sitting on the wall
by the bank stood up and said to Alvin, "You
should sue that woman. I'm a lawyer. I'll
represent you for nothing, just a percentage
of the award. It'll be fun. What do you say,
pal?" "I hate lawyers," Alvin said. "I do, too,"
the man said, and walked away. Alvin looked up
and saw the lady with the baby carriage
charging him as fast as she could run. She looked
completely deranged. The baby was smiling.
People were leaping to get out of her way.
Alvin thought, she's fast, she's mean. She won't
stop until the job is done. I like that, I like
that a lot. My, my the town is really rocking
on this beautiful summer's morn.

Holy Saturday

I came out of the store, and the first thing I saw
was a man in a bunny suit dancing down the sidewalk, handing
out chocolate eggs to everyone. Never take candy from strangers
was the first thing that leapt to mind. I wanted to reach the
car before he caught up with me. He saw this, and took a giant
hop in my direction. "Here, this is for you, Mr. Get-away-as-
fast-as-you-can," he said. "I don't want it," I said. "I'm
allergic to chocolate." He made a fist with his paw and threatened
my nose. "Take it," he said, "you can give it to a child, and
they will thank you." "I don't know any children, and, besides,
how do I know there isn't arsenic in there. I don't know you.
You're a complete stranger to me. You might be an escaped convict,
a child molester, or a murderer." "I'm the Easter bunny, you
asshole. If you can't trust the Easter bunny, you're in pretty
bad shape. Take the egg before I shove it down your throat,"
he said. I grabbed him by the shoulders and threw him up against
my car. The whiskers on his nose were twitching. His long,
floppy ears looked pathetic. "You are about to become a
very wounded bunny," I said. "Maybe we could talk this over, over a
beer or something. What do you say?" the bunny said. A couple
of teenagers had gathered to see what I might do next. They
were excited. I, who've never been in a fight, really wanted
to punch the bunny. But, instead, I dragged him off the car.
I took his basket out of his paw and threw it in a trash can.
"Now go home and get out of that suit. There's enough crime
in this town without you impersonating the Easter bunny and
handing out suspicious substances to little children," I said.
"I was trying to do a good thing," he said. "I was trying to
bring a little cheer and good will, that's all." "But you've
got a bunny suit on, for god's sake. And you were dancing on
the sidewalk like an idiot. Why should anyone trust you?" I
said. "Let's rip that suit off of him and see who he really is,"
one of the teenagers said. The bunny looked really frightened.
He was half-bent over, as if about to hop. "No," I said, "I
think he's learned his lesson." The boys seemed disappointed,
and I was starting to worry about the safety of the bunny.
"Get in the car," I said to him. "What?" he said. "I said,

get in the car. I'll drive you home." I unlocked the car, and
got into the driver's seat. The bunny seemed confused, but did
as I had said. He told me where he lived, and we drove there
in silence. He lived in a run-down apartment complex. Half
the domestic crime in town took place right there. When I
stopped, he started to open the door. He looked so defeated.
"What do you do, I mean, in real life?" I said. "I'm unemployed
right now," he said. "Every time I get a job, the place closes
down. It's like I'm the kiss of death." Hearing this from a
raggedy-assed Easter bunny should have been funny, but it wasn't.
It nearly broke my heart. "I'm sorry I ruined your day. Honestly,
I don't know what came over me. Maybe I was envious of your
happiness," I said. "That's what's great about the bunny suit,"
he said, "no one can see your tears. Thanks for the ride. After
nearly killing me, you saved my life. Makes a perfect story.
Unfortunately, I've got no one to tell it to." He got out of
the car and started hopping across the little, gravelly yard.
I never even saw his face or got his name.

The Formal Invitation

I was invited to a formal dinner party given by Marguerite Farnish
Burridge and her husband, Knelm Oswald Lancelot Burridge. I
had never met either of them, and had no idea why I was invited.
When the butler announced me, Mrs. Burridge came up and greeted me
quite graciously. "I'm so happy you could join us," she said.
"I know Knelm is looking forward to talking to you later." "I
can't wait," I said, "I mean, the pleasure's all mine." Nothing
came out right. I wanted to escape right then, but Mrs. Burridge
dragged me and introduced me to some of her friends. "This is
Nicholas and Sondra Pepperdene. Nicholas is a spy," she said.
"I am not," he said. "Yes, you are, darling. Everyone knows it,"
she said. "And Sondra does something with swans, I'm not
sure what. She probably mates them, knowing Sondra." "Really!
I'm saving them from extinction," Mrs. Pepperdene said. "And this
is Mordecai Rhinelander, and, as you might guess from his name,
he's a Nazi. And his wife, Dagmar, is a Nazi, too. Still, lovely
people," she said. "Marguerite, you're giving our new friend
a very bad impression," Mr. Rhinelander said. "Oh, it's my party
and I can say what I want," Mrs. Burridge said. A servant was
passing with cocktails and she grabbed two off the tray and handed
me one. "I hope you like martinis," she said, and left me standing
there. "My name is Theodore Fullerton," I said, "and I'm a depraved
jazz musician. I prey on young women, take drugs whenever possible,
but most of the time I just sleep all day and am out of work."
They looked at one another, and then broke out laughing. I smiled
like an idiot and sipped my drink. I thought it was going to be
an awful party, but I just told the truth whenever I was spoken
to, and people thought I was hilariously funny. At dinner, I was
seated between Carmen Milanca and Godina Barnafi. The first course was
fresh crabmeat on a slice of kiwi. Mine managed to slip off the
plate and landed in the lap of Carmen Milanca. She had on a
very tight, short black dress. She smiled at me, waiting to see
what I would do. I reached over and plucked it from its nest.
"Nice shot," she said. "It was something of a bull's-eye, wasn't
it?" I said. Godina Barnafi asked me if I found wealthy women
to be sexy. "Oh yes, of course," I said, "but I generally prefer
poor, homeless waifs, you know, runaways, mentally addled,

unwashed, sickly, starving women." "Fascinating," she said. A leg of lamb was served. Knelm Burridge proposed a toast. "To my good friends gathered here tonight, and to your great achievements in the further-ance of peace on Earth." I still had no idea what I was doing there. I mentioned this to Carmen since we'd almost been intimate. "You're probably the sacrificial lamb," she said. "The what?" I said. "The human sacrifice, you know, to the gods, for peace," she said. "I figure it's got to be you, because I recognize all the rest of them, and they're friends." "You've got to be kidding me," I said. "No, we all work for peace in our various ways, and then once a year we get together and have this dinner." "But why me?" I said. "That's Marguerite's job. She does the research all year, and she tries to pick someone who won't be missed, someone who's not giving in a positive way to society, someone who is essentially selfish. Her choices are very carefully considered and fair, I think, though I am sorry it's you this time. I think I could get to like you," she said. I picked at my food. "Well, I guess I was a rather good choice, except that some people really like my music. They even say it heals them," I said. "I'm sure it does," Carmen said, "but Marguerite takes everything into consideration. She's very thorough."

When I went out to weed my garden, I found a wild
baby in it. It snarled at me, and I ran. I had read that
they were becoming a problem in this part of the state. No
one knew where they came from, but they were known to be
incredibly quick and vicious. I went back in the house
and locked the door. Through the kitchen window, I watched
it eat a dozen tomatoes. Then it threw up, and started
eating more. It was a disgusting little creature. The
article I had read advised shooting them on sight "to stop
the epidemic." The creature was eating my flowers by the
fistful. Then it rolled around in the dirt, laughing.
I dialed 911 and reported the wild baby. "Stay in your house.
Do not leave your house," the woman said. Two minutes
later there was a squad car in my driveway. The officers
got out with their shotguns. I didn't want to watch the
slaughter, so I went into the living room and picked up the
paper, but, of course, I couldn't read. I waited tensely
for the explosions. I waited and waited, but there were none.
I went to the kitchen window and looked around. There were
no officers in sight, and no wild baby. I walked around
the house, peering through each window. Nothing, save for
the police car in my driveway with its cherry light still
turning. Of course I had been told not to leave the house
under any circumstances, but this was too much. I didn't own
a gun, so I grabbed a long, sharp kitchen knife. Near the
garden, the grass was stained with blood, and there was
evidence of a tremendous struggle. I was shaking as I
prowled around the house. I figured the baby had eaten the
two policemen and would now be quite huge, but perhaps it
would be sleepy, too, after such a giant meal. It couldn't
still be hungry, or was I kidding myself? I finished circling
the house without incident. The officers were sitting on my
door stoop having a smoke. "I thought that thing had eaten
both of you," I said. "Nice place you've got here," one of
them said. "That wasn't a real wild baby," the other one
said. "That was just a baby someone didn't want. They're
a dime a dozen. Most of them learn to get by on their own,

but, of course, some don't make it." "What about the blood in the yard?" I said. "It took a bite out of my ankle, nothing serious," he said. "And where did it go?" I asked. "It was too fast. We didn't see where it went. It will probably be back, but it's nothing to worry about," he said. "But it's my home," I said. "I need to feel safe, my garden." "Share the bounty," the first officer said. "You've got plenty to go around. They're only babies, you know."

Fatty told Smiley that Slim was getting
on his nerves. Slim told Smiley to mind his
own business. Smiley said, "This is my business,
because you and Fatty are my two best friends."
Red said, "What about me, Smiley, aren't I one
of your best friends, too?" "Of course you are,
Red. I'm just trying to patch things up between
Slim and Fatty. Friends like them shouldn't
be fighting," Smiley said. "I'm not fighting
with Fatty. He's fighting with me," Slim said.
"You called me Fatty the fatty," Fatty said.
"Well, if you can't take a joke, it's not my
fault," Slim smirked. "Come on, boys," Smiley
said, "can't you hear yourselves bickering like
a couple of old maids. Why don't you shake hands
and make up and stop all this name calling."
"Can I shake hands, too?" Red said. "I don't
want to shake hands with Red," Fatty said. Slim
said, "Red once called me a beanpole." "I did
not," Red said. "I said you resembled a bean-
pole." "You boys are making my smile droop,"
Smiley said. "See what we've gone and done,"
Fatty said. "It's a bad day when Smiley's
smile droops," Slim added. "I never even had
a smile," Red sighed. "Let's make up, Slim,"
Fatty proposed. "Oh, alright," Slim said,
shaking Fatty's hand. "Warriors in the pursuit
of the higher truths, always searching, seeking,
embracing, never shirking, for the soul is
fashioned by love and we are ever marching
toward it," Smiley said. "Wow," Red said.
"Amazing," Fatty said. "Are you alright,
Smiley?" Slim inquired. "A tad . . . wan," he said,
and then his legs buckled, and he collapsed.
Red ran around in circles, squeaking. "He'll
be alright," Fatty said. "He's just resting
for the long march." "Marching hurts my feet,"

Slim said. "I'm not going on any long march. And, besides, Smiley wasn't in his right mind when he made that speech." "Mr. Know-it-all," Fatty said, "Mrs. Lazy, Mr. Too-good-to-march. Mr. Twiggy."

Intruders

It was around midnight, and I knew something
was out in the yard. I hadn't heard anything, I
just felt it. It was a cloudy night, no stars
shone through. Every now and then a bit of the
moon would peek through. I walked around, shining
my flashlight up and down the yard. Frogs croaked
at intervals, and other night creatures scurried
over the leaves. I knew something else was present
nearby. Finally, my flashlight caught the face of
a man standing on the far edge of my property.
I think I frightened him more than he frightened
me. "What are you doing here?" I said in a slightly
harsh voice. "My wife kicked me out. I had nowhere
to go. I live down the street in the trailer.
My name's Daryl," he said. "Well, that's a pretty
rough story, Daryl," I said, "but if I had a gun
I'd have to shoot you. I just can't have a stranger
roaming around my property at night." "I understand,"
he said. "Here, you can have my gun." "You have
a gun?" I said. "It's legal," he said. "I'm a
security guard. You can have it. Go ahead, shoot
me." "Daryl, I have no interest in the world in
shooting you." The moon came out just then, and
I could see his face. He was just a kid, and he'd
obviously been crying. "I love her," he said,
"but she's got big ideas, and I guess I'm just not
good enough for her." She was nearby. I could
sense her sneaking up on us. Whether she, too,
was armed or coming to reconcile, I had no idea.
I whispered to Daryl, "Give me the gun."

I got a call from the White House, from the
president himself, asking me if I'd do him a personal
favor. I like the president, so I said, "Sure, Mr.
President, anything you like." He said, "Just act
like nothing's going on. Act normal. That would
mean the world to me. Can you do that, Leon?" "Why,
sure, Mr. President, you've got it. Normal, that's
how I'm going to act. I won't let on, even if I'm
tortured," I said, immediately regretting that "tortured"
bit. He thanked me several times and hung up. I was
dying to tell someone that the president himself called
me, but I knew I couldn't. The sudden pressure to
act normal was killing me. And what was going on
anyway. I didn't know anything was going on. I
saw the president on TV yesterday. He was shaking
hands with a farmer. What if it wasn't really a
farmer? I needed to buy some milk, but suddenly
I was afraid to go out. I checked what I had on.
I looked "normal" to me, but maybe I looked more
like I was trying to be normal. That's pretty
suspicious. I opened the door and looked around.
What was going on? There was a car parked in front
of my car that I had never seen before, a car that
was trying to look normal, but I wasn't fooled.
If you need milk, you have to get milk, otherwise
people will think something's going on. I got into
my car and sped down the road. I could feel those
little radar guns popping behind every tree and bush,
but, apparently, they were under orders not to stop
me. I ran into Kirsten in the store. "Hey, what's
going on, Leon?" she said. She had a very nice smile.
I hated to lie to her. "Nothing's going on. Just
getting milk for my cat," I said. "I didn't know
you had a cat," she said. "I meant to say coffee.
You're right, I don't have a cat. Sometimes I
refer to my coffee as my cat. It's just a private
joke. Sorry," I said. "Are you all right?" she

asked. "Nothing's going on, Kirsten. I promise you. Everything is normal. The president shook hands with a farmer, a real farmer. Is that such a big deal?" I said. "I saw that," she said, "and that man was definitely not a farmer." "Yeah, I know," I said, feeling better.

After we came out of the Chinese restaurant,
I said to Dana, "Did you notice anything funny in
there?" "Yeah, there was a man in the back dressed
like a samurai warrior staring at us as though he
wanted to kill us." "Exactly. But we've been going
there for years. They know us. I was worried we
weren't going to make it out of there. What do you
think's going on?" We were walking briskly away from
Chen's. "Maybe they're being held captive. Maybe
some kind of Chinese mafia has taken them over," she
said. "Maybe we should go to the police. They'd
probably think we were crazy," I said. "The Chens
are such nice people. I'd hate it if anything happened
to them," she said. We both stopped walking. "Let's
go back. I'll say I lost a glove or something. We'll
try to talk to one of them," I said. Dana agreed.
Madame Chen gave her usual big smile when we entered.
I pulled her aside and whispered into her ear, "Are
you in trouble? Do you need help?" She looked
wildly perplexed. "No, no, we are very fine. Why
do you ask such a question?" she said. "The samurai
warrior in back," I said. "We thought he was going
to kill us. We worried that you were in danger,"
Dana added. "Ohhh," she said, "that is my son. He
is back from college. Such a big boy. He likes to
dress up when he is home. He's the only Chinese boy
at school, you see." I looked up and there he was
staring at us from the back room with murder in his
eye. "Well, we just wanted to make sure everything
was fine. Sorry for the misunderstanding," Dana said.
We bowed and left the restaurant. I felt an incredible
sadness in my heart. We didn't speak all the way back
to the car. And then, Dana said, "I guess there's

nothing we can do." "They're submitting to their
fate. It's hard to fight with that. I'm sure in
their world it's noble and wise. We're just customers.
We know nothing and we never will," I said. "Let's
go home. Mrs. Chen wouldn't want us to cry."

Shiloh

On Monday, Miss Francis told her sixth-grade
class that she was getting married soon. The class
was very happy for her, and they asked her lots of
questions about her wedding plans. They never once
mentioned the Civil War. On Tuesday, she came in
late wiping tears from her eyes, and told them
there was going to be no wedding. The class let out
a collective sigh. They tried to console her through-
out the hour. No one mentioned Appomattox. On Wed-
nesday, she surprised them all by announcing that the
wedding would, indeed, take place, and that it was
going to be bigger and fancier than originally planned.
The class cheered and applauded. They wanted to know
all the details. She drew a picture of her gown on
the blackboard. She told them all about the food
and the music. Little Rory sat in the back of the
class listening, but what he saw was Pickett's charge
up the ridge at Gettysburg, the mayhem and slaughter,
the horse shot and collapsing, a total of 51,000 dead.
And four months later, Lincoln's great speech at the
cemetery, 267 words, given in four minutes. Rory knew
the speech by heart, and was saying it to himself,
barely able to hold back tears, when Rebecca Crothers
had the impertinency to ask Miss Francis if she was a
virgin. "Long ago and far away," Miss Francis replied.
Rory pictured her camped beside the battlefield,
nervously waiting for her man, who would never return.

The Interview

A man named Mr. Fazenda called me and said
he was an agent and he would like to ask me a few
questions. I told him I would be happy to answer
any questions he might have for me. "Do you know
a woman by the name of Geraldine Morgan?" he said.
"Well, I've only met her a few times," I said. "Still,
do you think she would be willing to betray her country?"
he asked. "Well, sure, I think she'd be willing to
do that," I said. "Do you think she's capable of
murder?" he said. "From what little I know of her,
I think she's definitely capable of that," I said.
"Would she harm the president if she had an oppor-
tunity?" he asked. "As I said, I barely know her,
but I imagine she would take advantage of that
opportunity," I said. And then I added, "I hope
I'm not causing any trouble for Miss Morgan, because,
really, I quite like her, even though she appears
to be something of a slut and a lush." "Oh, no, no,
Mr. Sanderson. Miss Morgan is being considered for
a job here at the agency, and your answers have been
quite helpful."

In a Past Life

This man named Gordon came over to me at
a party last week and said he had known me in
a previous life. "You were a shepherd," he
said. "Oh yeah," I said, "that sounds nice."
"Actually," he said, "you were a crime boss
pretending to be a shepherd." "That doesn't
sound like something I'd do," I said. "Yeah,"
he said, "but you were very good to your six
children and two wives." "Two wives?" I said.
"You had other people do all the killing," he
said. "So basically a nice guy, right?" I
said. "Except if somebody crossed you. Then,
look out, there's nothing you wouldn't do, cut
off fingers, gouge eyeballs," he said. "You're
really full of shit," I said. And I made a
move as if to poke his eyes out. He jumped
back, terrified. "You're definitely him," he
said. "All that's a long time ago," I said.
And I held my hand out to him, "Come on, let
me get you a drink." "But I was just making
that stuff up," he said. "I wasn't," I said.

Not Long Ago, Milk Cows Ruminated There

There are new buildings going up all over
town, big buildings, and I don't know what any
are going to be, and it frightens me. And the
curious thing is that nobody mentions them, not
a word. It's as if they don't see them. And
there's nothing in the paper about them. One
day I'm driving down Route 9 and there are three
buildings going up. A couple of days later there
are six. A few days after that there are nine.
They're spreading like spores, but they're huge.
They all lack character, they lack design. And
as they near completion, it becomes clear that
secrecy and security and anonymity are their main
objectives. No sign goes up announcing their
company's name. No job openings are advertised.
No cars are seen coming and going. I guess it's
the New World, arrived without even a peep, and
someone thinks it's best that we know nothing
about it. Masked men with titanium pincers slide
silently through the blackened halls.

Thanks to the new beaver dam, Mr. Foley's
yard was flooding. He was furious and called
the police. Officer Crothers stood there, shaking
his head. "It's a real beauty, isn't it?" he said.
"But it's flooding my yard, and soon it will be
in my basement," Mr. Foley said. "Well, there's
nothing we can do about it. They're protected,
and you'd pay a very stiff fine, and possibly
do time in jail if you so much as ruffled the
fur of one of them," Crothers said. "You mean
a beaver is more important than a man, than my
whole family?" Mr. Foley said. "I didn't say
that. I didn't make the law, I just enforce it.
The beavers didn't think they were building a
dam, you know. It's their home. They've got
wives and kids, too. They've got grandparents,
and aunts and uncles. They might even have little
beaver TV sets for all I know. Let them be,
Mr. Foley. Let them be." Officer Crothers
started to walk away. "One hand grenade right
in the middle of it is all it would take," Mr.
Foley said. Crothers stopped and looked Foley
in the eye. "After four hundred years of slaughter,
we're finally at peace with the beavers. They're
happy, and we're happy. They're hard working,
intelligent and strong. Have you got a problem
with that, Mr. Foley?" "But my yard is flooding,"
Mr. Foley said. "For god's sake, pretend you're
a beaver. That's what the rest of us do,"
Crothers said.

Love Child

In a little town south of here, a woman gave
birth to a wolf. Well, it wasn't exactly a wolf,
but a child that was evidently part wolf. It had
a hairy snout and furry, pointed ears. The woman's
name was Vannesa Holtz, and when she was questioned
about it, she admitted to having relations with a
certain wolf. She had been hiking in the hills, and,
at some point, she realized that she was being followed.
She seemed confused about the actual sequence of
events. All she said was, "He was beautiful and
gentle with me. I think he really loved me." Police
and doctors were baffled, and the child has been
locked in a special ward by itself, under guard.
While checking her background for irregularities,
the police discovered that I had dated her for a
period of two years. They came to interview me.
I admitted that she liked me to bite her, and they
acted like that was a big deal. Then I told them
that she was fond of saying that I was "part wolf."
That really excited them. I said that I thought
that the child might be mine. They said, "And are
you part wolf?" "Perhaps just a little, one-eighteenth,
if at all," I said. "That's not unusual," Officer
Pollack said. Officer Gilbert said, "I myself am
one-twelfth wolf, and I bite my wife all the time."
"Well, I guess we've cleared this matter up," Pollack
said. "What about the child?" I said. "If Miss
Holtz wants to join the pack, that's her business.
Right now, that seems to be where her heart is
leaning. We have no control in this matter,"
Gilbert said. "But what about me?" I said. "I
don't think you have what it takes," Pollack said,
baring his teeth and walking out the door.

Sleepy Visitation

I took a sip of water and looked around the
room. Everything was normal, the paintings, the
chairs, the sofa, the lamps, except there was this
man standing in the corner. He was not a threatening
presence, in fact, he was almost cowering, trying
to blend in. I walked over and sized him up. He
had on a bow tie and was trembling a bit, a small
man compared to me. "What are you doing here?" I
said. "Just resting," he said. "I've traveled
a great distance and am in need of a rest." "Well,
as long as you're quiet and don't go breaking any
lamps, a little rest will reinvigorate you," I said.
"Thank you, sir," he said. Then I went about my
business, straightening up the house and putting
things away. I completely forgot about the little
man in the corner. I sat in the same room with him
for quite some time without noticing him. Then,
I looked up from my book and was given quite a start.
"What are you doing here?" I said. "I'm still
resting," he said. "Oh, yes," I said, "I'm sorry
if I disturbed you." "Not at all," he said. I
went back to reading my book. It was a brutal
mystery novel and I was deeply absorbed in it,
so that when I looked up again I screamed. The
little man himself screamed, too. "What are you
doing here?" I shouted. "I was trying to rest, but
I can see that is quite impossible. In my poor,
debilitated condition I shall have to move on," he
said. A wave of shame and pity overcame me. "Oh,
please forgive me," I said. "I promise I'll be
better. Stay for dinner, and you can sleep in my
bed this evening. Your health is foremost of my
concerns." "No one will let me rest. You're no
different than the others. You mean well, I know
that. I have circled the globe, and it's always
the same. I wish to hurt no one. In fact, if only
I could get a little sleep, I think I would be

capable of great love and great good deeds. I
don't understand it, I don't understand it at all,"
he said. And then he walked out of the room and
opened the kitchen door. I jumped out of my chair
and ran after him, but he had disappeared into the
night. I kicked myself. How was I supposed to
know?

Elysium

I had been sitting under an apple tree
in a meadow not far from town, when I spotted
a bluebird. They're quite rare these days, at
least around here, so I was excited. It flew
around my head, and then landed on a branch above
me. I was musing on my good fortune when I noticed
another nearby, and that made me smile even more.
The midday sun lulled me into an unexpected nap.
I'm not sure how long I dozed, but when I awoke
there were dozens of bluebirds darting and alighting
all about me. I was giddy with delight and almost
disbelief. Never in my dreams had I seen such a
congregation of delicately hued creatures. They
seemed to be flirting with me, swarming about my
head and shoulders, grazing my cheeks with the tips
of their wings. They were so playful and friendly,
I was not surprised when several of them landed
on the top of my head. I sat there, mesmerized.
But through the haze of blue in front of me, something
else was going on, something even stranger. Two
men in silver jumpsuits with gas masks were climbing
the hill toward me. They had powerpacks on their
backs, and were carrying long hoses or flamethrowers,
I couldn't tell which. The bluebirds continued to
flutter before my eyes, and I was suddenly consumed
by an hallucinatory fear. The men kept trudging
toward me with all their bulky equipment. My heart
was pounding. Then suddenly, there was this horrible
sucking sound, almost deafening. It lasted about
fifteen seconds, but felt much longer. The men
took off their masks and all was quiet. "Soul-suckers,"
one of them said. "What?" I said. "They look like
bluebirds, but they're really Soul-suckers. The ones
on your head were sucking your soul. We may have
gotten them just in time. Or they may have succeeded
in getting just part of your soul," he said. "There's
a device down at headquarters that can assess the loss

if you'd like to know," the other one said. I was
still feeling disoriented. I stood up, but my legs
shook. I started to ask them how they knew I was
there, but didn't. "I'll be alright," I said. "And
thanks for the good work." I started walking. Even
a part of my so-called soul inhabiting those bluebirds
for just a few moments before their untimely end thrilled
me beyond words. I felt like a wild balloon in the wind
filled with secrets.

Why We Must Sleep

One night I met Harvey in the middle of a
misty field. We had made some plan, but I had
pretty much forgotten what it was, I just knew I
was supposed to meet him there. Each of us was
carrying a small, brown paper bag. I could barely
make Harvey out in the mist. He looked like a ghost.
"What's in your bag?" I said. He held the bag up
to his eyes and looked. "Just some buttons and
safety pins and a glass eye," he said. "Could be
some jelly beans, too, I'm not sure." "Well, it
sounds like we're set," I said. "Did you bring
what you were supposed to bring?" he asked. I
tried to look into my bag. "I don't know," I said.
"I think I've got some rubber bands and a crayon and
some sunflower seeds and a compass." "Excellent,"
he said. "There's a big pine tree over there about
a hundred yards from here. You can see the top of
it above the mist. Let's head for that." It was
past midnight, and I was sleepy, but I tried to wake
myself up thinking of the fun we were going to have.
Harvey specialized in fun. We started walking, but
my legs were heavy. I was dragging them like sacks
of lead. "What's the matter, old boy?" Harvey said.
"I'll catch up with you. Don't worry about me," I
said. I lost sight of Harvey. Then I stumbled on
a rock, and my arms flailed out, and I threw my paper
bag up into the air. I got down on my knees and
started crawling around with a sense of desperation.
I would never find the sunflower seeds, that was for
sure, but there was a chance I could find the other
items. I felt like a blind dog, except I couldn't
even sniff. I crawled and crawled, and finally I
found the empty bag. Joy and despair alternately
filled my heart. Harvey was gone. I could neither
hear nor see him. He had forgotten me. I continued
searching, fighting off sleep, trying to keep hope
alive. My back ached, my arms hurt. My fingers sifted

through the grass like a mad detective. When I eventually
found the compass, it was stuck in some foul jelly
and reeked of death. I was terrified of touching it
a second time, and crawled away as fast as I could.
I wanted to go home. I wanted to sleep in my own bed.
But then the moon started to come out. I stood up and
stretched. Harvey was standing there. "It's okay, Gus.
I lost everything, too. Maybe someday we'll pull it off.
I think a moose butted me out there, just as I was in the
homestretch. I hated losing that glass eye. It had been
my lucky charm since I was a kid," he said. "I'm sorry,"
I said, "but a moose means you're blessed for life."
"Then it was all worth it," he said.

I Never Meant to Harm Him

I was sitting at my desk in my second-floor
study when this helicopter pulled right up to the
window. A man was leaning out of it shouting some-
thing at me, but of course I couldn't hear a word.
I went to the window and opened it. It was still
almost impossible to hear anything over the roar of
the engine and the whir of the blades. I kept shouting,
"What? I can't hear you." "Let the boy go!" he said.
"I don't have any boy in here," I said. "Let him go,"
he said. "There's no boy in here," I said. "You've
made some kind of mistake. I don't have any boy." I
shouted. They finally flew away and one of them waved
to me. I went back to work, somewhat rattled. It took
me a while to regain my concentration. I was plotting
my trip down the Amazon, but now when I pictured me
paddling the dugout canoe, I also saw a small boy
nestled in there, sometimes sleeping, other times
pointing out large water snakes near us. The boy
seemed very familiar to me, but, in truth, I knew not
who he was. As the days and nights passed into weeks,
our supplies dwindled. The rain forests were full of
unimaginable sounds, screeches and hollerings during
the night that made sleep almost impossible. The boy
was brave, but rarely spoke. He stared at me with his
big, brown eyes. He trusted me with his life, but more
and more I had no idea how we were going to get out
of there, or why we had come. At one point, several
naked Indians stood on the shore with their blowguns
and watched us pass. I wanted to ask for help, but
was afraid for the boy. It was so hot and humid I
was nearly delirious. The boy dozed during the worst
of it. I had no memory of kidnapping him, but where
did he come from? The crocodiles eyed us lazily, but
they're not lazy, they're sly. I've seen them snap up
a tapir or an anteater in a flash. One mistake and
you're lunch. Somewhere there's a rivertown where we
can replenish our supplies, but, as it turns out, the

map is unreliable. Whose boy is this? I never meant
to harm him. He's beautiful but we're drifting. I
have no strength. Surely he can see that. It was our
destiny all along. The sun, the river, and then the night.
And then nothing. "It's okay," he said, "I like being
with you. We're having fun."

A Trout in the Tam o' Shanter

I was walking out of the fish market when
a man on a bicycle came speeding by and nearly hit
me. He wasn't going to stop and apologize, so I
reached in my bag and fired a trout at his head,
narrowly missing. I started running after him
and threw another trout. This one hit the mark,
and he crashed into a parked car. He struggled
to his feet, badly hurt. His bike was a crumpled
mess. The fish lay beside it needing a little
rinse. "What the hell do you think you're doing?"
he said. "You nearly killed me." "And, you, sir,
nearly ran me down back there," I said. "You've
destroyed my bike." It was then that he noticed
the fish. "My god, you're insane! You hit me
with a fish," he said. "I want that fish back,
that's my supper." When I approached him, he looked
frightened. He was wearing a tam o' shanter, which
made me want to hit him again. "You're not going
to hit me again?" he said. "I just want my fish,"
I said. "My hat smells like fish," he said, holding
it sadly in his hands. "I'm sorry about your bike,"
I said. "Perhaps it can be fixed," he said. "It
is old and dear to me." His pants and coat were
threadbare, and his shoes had seen their better day.
"I believe it's my responsibility to bear the cost
of all repairs," I said. "I insist on it." His
eyes went watery as he replaced his foolish hat.
He wiped his eyes with his sleeve. "You missed
with the first one, didn't you?" he said. "What?"
I said. "The first fish. I saw it fly past me. I
was pretty excited, knew something big was up, like
a whole new day. And, then, whack, and I was smashed
into this car." "Oh, yes, I missed with the first
one. But the second one was perfect, right on target,"

I said. "Do you often attack old men with your fish?"
he said. "You're my very first," I said. He reflected
on that for a while, then said, "Perhaps we should
celebrate to mark the occasion." And that is how my
friendship with Jacob Faversham began.

Swoon

One of Daniela's breasts fell out of her blouse
during dinner in our favorite restaurant. I liked
looking at it and didn't say anything. The waiter
liked looking at it, too, and just smiled. The other
diners tried not to stare, but some of the men couldn't
help themselves. Daniela takes a certain pride in her
breasts, so perhaps it wasn't an accident. I knew I
should say something to her, but I was also getting
really turned on. It was as if I had never met this
woman before. The public aspect of breast exposure
had a mystery to it that I couldn't name. I said,
"The fileto tre pepe was exceptionally good tonight."
I stared at her breast as if it were about to speak.
"The gnocchi was delicious," it said. "You're looking
especially beautiful tonight," I said. "It's good
to get out and see the people," it said. Daniela
had gone into a swoon or trance of some kind, and the
breast had taken over. When the waiter came for the
bill, he said to Daniela's breast, "Very nice to see you tonight."
The breast blushed, gently swaying in the candlelight.

The Historical Society

Rick dragged me to a meeting of the Historical
Society, in which he'd been an active member for the
past five years. There were about twenty people in
attendance, most of them in their eighties. It seems
there had been an unsolved murder in our town two hundred
and fifty years ago, and these folks were trying to
solve it now. They eyed me suspiciously, as though I
might somehow have been involved. One little old lady
spoke furiously, "It was that slut, Mehitable Nims, who
killed Benoni Stebbins. She had been sleeping with him
for three years, and he still wouldn't leave his wife.
When you read her letters, you can feel her anger mounting.
He had no other enemies. People just didn't believe a
woman could be that savage." "Oh, Elizabeth, you read
sex into everything. People kill for other reasons,
too. Such as money. We don't really know if he was
robbed. He might have had a lot of money, or gold,
around. The records don't really tell us that," an old
man with a white beard said. Rick glanced at me to see
if I was finding this interesting. I smiled back. "Martha
French was sleeping with Mehitable Nims, I might add, if
this is of interest to anyone. Those of you with weak
stomachs may care to leave the room," Elizabeth added
with an air of triumph. "And Benoni Stebbins was also
sleeping with Martha. Now who do you think murdered him?"
A woman with a large white bun of hair with a pencil stuck
through it said, "I think you murdered him, Elizabeth."
She chuckled at her own devilishness. "Oh, no, I quite
admire Benoni. He was apparently quite the stud. I know
more than I'm willing to share with you today," Elizabeth
said smugly. "It seems to me that Martha French should
be a suspect, too," Rick said. "No, no, she was very happy
with the arrangement, I can assure you. She loved both
of her lovers. Well, I shouldn't say both, because there
were more. There was Captain Holson and the Reverend
Frary and Catherine Ducharme, to name a few. She was a
very generous woman," Elizabeth said. People were eyeing

Elizabeth, as though she knew just a little too much about what went on in people's bedrooms two hundred and fifty years ago. Elizabeth sat there staring into space, righteously proud of her knowledge. "What do you think, young man?" someone said to me. "It could be Benoni's wife. No one's mentioned her," I said. "It's true, she was long-suffering," an old lady with a lace collar said. "Long-suffering," several others repeated. "He's a bright young man," someone said. "Can we have some coffee and donuts now," someone said. Several had dozed off and were snoring. Rick came over to me and said, "Do you want to join up and become a member? We meet the third Wednesday of every month." "It seems like you have to spend an awful lot of time doing research," I said. "Are you kidding? They just make all this stuff up," he said. "No," I said, "it was all true. And it was Benoni's wife. I'd bet my life on it."

The Wild Turkey

I was standing at the kitchen sink washing
a few dishes, when I hear this knocking at my door.
I looked out the window, but there was no one there.
But the knocking continued. I looked down, and there
was this wild turkey staring at me. He must have been
about four feet tall, and he was looking right into
my eyes. Then he pecked at the door again, and I
instinctively opened it. He walked into the middle
of the room and said, "Gobble gobble gobble." I poured
him a bowl of dry cereal and another bowl of water.
He tried the cereal and seemed to like it. He'd take
four or five bites, and then wash it all down with a
couple of sips of water. Then he'd look up at me
with his blue head and his red and white mottled neck.
He finished the cereal, then flapped his great wings
as if to thank me. His green iridescent feathers
glazed the room in a magical light. I walked into
the living room, and he followed me. I sat down in my
chair, and he leapt up on the back of the couch. He had
the meekest, almost beseeching eyes, that seemed to
say, "Whatever you want to do next is fine by me.
I'm your guest, after all, and we've only just met,
though I feel like I've known you for a lifetime,
old friend, new friend, good friend." "Gobble gobble
gobble," I said. He didn't reply, but turned his head
away and stared at the TV, which was off. We sat there
in silence for a good long time. Sometimes our eyes
met, and we'd wander down those ancient hallways, a
little afraid, a little in awe. And then we'd turn away
having reached a locked door. He studied the room, too,
for any clue, but it must have all seemed so alien,
the beautiful vases and bowls, the paintings, scraps
of a lost civilization. Hours passed like this. I felt
an immense calm within me. We were sleeping in a tree
on an island in an unknown land.

A woman knocked on my door and introduced herself
as Loreen Flockerzie. "I'm sorry to disturb you," she
said, "but I was wondering if you could tell me how to
get to the Peace Pagoda from here." "It's not far from
here," I said, and gave her directions. "The Buddhists
won't try to enslave me or anything, will they?" she said.
"I don't think that's their kind of thing," I said. "But,
of course, I could be wrong." She was craning her neck
trying to look around my kitchen. "One of my best friends
is a slave to a prince in Thailand. The things she's had
to do you wouldn't believe," she said. "Mind if I have
a glass of water? It's hot as blazes out here." "Come in,"
I said. "I'll get you some ice water." "It's so much cooler
in here," she said, looking around. "I bet you live alone.
It's such a masculine house." "Well, actually, I have a
slave," I said. Loreen Flockerzie's eyes lit up. "You
do?" she exclaimed. "I do," I said. "I keep her chained
in the basement when I'm not using her." "That makes sense,"
she said. "Tell me, have you ever had more than one at a
time?" "Oh yes, I've had as many as a hundred, but it makes
for an awful mess," I said. Loreen was now wandering around
the house freely. "Oh yes, I can see that that would be
a problem," she said. "The poor women at the Peace Pagoda
live in terrible squalor, I'm told." "The monks are brutal
to them," I said, "beatings with bamboo poles." "You'd
think the authorities would do something about it," she said.
"The police are afraid of the monks. They can put them into
trances and turn them into beetles," I said. She collapsed
onto my sofa. Heaving a sigh, she said, "I just wanted to
go there to pray for world peace." "That's what they all
say," I said. Loreen Flockerzie looked exhausted, and I was
afraid she might start crying on me. "Listen," I said, "there
are no women up there. They're monks, for god's sake. And
I don't have a slave in the basement, either. I was just
having a little fun with you." "You want to have a little
fun with me?" she said. "No, no, I didn't mean it that way,"
I said. "You captured me, fair and square," she said. "I

did not capture you," I said. "Regardless of what you say, I'm here. I fell for the old cool glass of water trick," she said. "You asked for the glass of water," I reminded her. "And you gave it to me. You lured me into your den of iniquity," she said. "The Peace Pagoda is really a lovely place, and I think you should go visit it right now," I said. "As you wish, master," she said. She stood and bowed and bowed again and again as she slowly made her way to the door.

The Rules

A man came into the store and said, "I'd like to
have two steaks, about ten ounces each, a half-an-inch
thick, please." I said, "Sir, this is a candy store.
We don't have steaks." He said, "And I'd like to have
two potatoes and a bunch of asparagus." I said, "I'm
sorry, this is a candy store, sir. That's all we carry."
He said, "I don't mind waiting." "It could be many years,"
I said. "I have plenty of time," he said. And, while he
was waiting, a woman came in and said, "Where is your hat
section? I'm hoping you have a large, red hat with a feather."
"I'm awfully sorry, but this is a candy store," I said. "We
don't carry hats." "I'd like to see it, nonetheless," she
said. "It might just fit me." "We only carry candy," I
said. "It might just fit me, anyway," she said. "If you'd
like to wear a piece of candy on your head, I could possibly
find something in red," I said. "That would be lovely,"
she said. And, then, another man came in and pulled out
a gun. "Give me all your money," he said. I said, "I'm
sorry, this is a candy store. We don't do hold ups."
"But I have a gun," he said. "Yes, I can see that, sir,
but it doesn't work in here. This is a candy store," I
said. He looked at the man and woman standing in the corner.
"What about them, can I hold them up?" he said. "Oh no,
I'm afraid not. They're covered under the candy store
protection plan, even though, technically, they don't know
they're in a candy store," I said. "Well, at least I knew
you were a candy store, I just didn't know there were all
these special rules. Can I at least have some jellybeans?
I'll pay you for them, don't worry," he said. As I was getting
him his jellybeans, another man walked in with a gun. "This
is a stickup," he said. "Give me all of your cash." The
first thief said, "This is a candy store, you fool. They
don't do stickups." "What do you mean, they don't do stickups?"
the second thief said. "It's against the rules," the first
one said. "I never read the rule book. I didn't even know
there was one," the second one said. "Would you like some
chocolate kisses, or perhaps some peanut brittle?" I said,

hoping to avert a squabble. He replaced the gun into his shoulder holster and scanned the glass cases thoughtfully. "A half-a-dozen chocolate-covered cherries would make me a very happy man," he said. "That's what candy stores are for," I said. The two thieves left together, munching their candy and chatting about a mutual friend. And that's when Bonita Sennot and Halissa Delphin came in. Halissa was wearing a large, red hat with a feather in it. The woman in the corner leapt forward. "That's it! That's the very hat I want," she said, yanking the hat off Halissa's head. Halissa grabbed the lady's arm and threw her to the floor, retrieving her hat. Bonita ordered a bag of malted milk balls. The man in the corner helped the woman to her feet. "That's my hat," she whispered to him. "She's wearing my hat." Halissa invited me to have dinner with them. I said, "Great!"

Wendell

We found ourselves driving on a little road
we'd never even heard of. There was dense forest
on either side, rough land, with outcroppings of
huge boulders. And, yet, to our surprise, there
were houses built back in there. You could barely
see them in the dark woods. We drove for miles and
miles like this, with no idea where we were. "Who are
these people, and where do they work, if they work
at all?" Caitlin said. "They don't work," I said.
"They hunt and fish and chop a lot of wood for the
hard winters." We drove on and on, happy to be lost.
A whole world, not that far from our own, had remained
hidden from us all these years. Eventually, we came
to a little town by the name of Wendell. There were
attractive old homes with lawns. And there was a
large town common with a bandstand and a gazebo.
Caitlin asked me to pull over and park. The first
thing we saw was a woman walking down the street
cradling a baby fox. She was feeding it with a
baby bottle. I said to Caitlin, "There's something
a little strange about this place, but I like it."
We passed an old man sitting on a bench wearing a
white suit and vest with a straw boater. He said,
"I see we have visitors. I hope you'll find our
little town amusing." We smiled and walked on. We
were both thirsty, so we headed for the only commercial
establishment in town, a drug store called The Dove.
It was filled with products from my childhood, items
that had long ago disappeared. "This is eerie," I
whispered to Caitlin. "I love it," she said. The
proprietor was watching our every move. "We should
load up on this stuff. It's worth a fortune," I said.
"No, don't, Max. You'll look suspicious. Let's just
get something to drink, and get out of here," she said.
We found the antique drinks and took them to the counter.
The man said, "Where are you people from?" I told him
and he said, "Never heard of it." "It's only fifteen

miles south of here," I said. "Never heard of it,"
he said. We left the store and headed for the common.
A group of children stopped what they were doing when
they saw us. They walked over and circled us and stared
in silence. Finally, one of them said, "You're not one
of us, so what are you?" "We're people from the future,"
I said. "We mean no harm to your people. We've come
to tell you that it will be all right when you get there."
"But we just live in Wendell. We're not going anywhere.
Nothing changes here. The band plays every Friday night.
It plays the same songs every Friday night. We play the
same games over and over. We never tire of them. They're
the best games in the world," a very cute girl said.
"We've made a big mistake, sorry, wrong planet. Carry on,
as before," I said. We found our car and sped off into
the primeval darkness.

I made several quick phone calls to my contacts.
Then I made my rounds of the yard, inspecting under
the trees, the foundation of the house, and the lawn
itself. There was one peculiar mushroom that hadn't
been there yesterday, and a fallen wren's nest, very
suspicious since there had been no wind. I made a
note of it, and went back inside. I called Henry
Furtek and gave him my report. He told me to proceed
to the next stage. I opened a can of chicken barley
soup and set it to boil. I looked under my bed with
a flashlight. Dust babies conspiring in the night to
choke me. I poured the soup and let it cool for two
minutes, carefully placing some saltines beside it.
When I had finished eating, I called Justin Nadworny
to tell him of my progress. "You're not out of the
thicket yet," he said. "I'm right in the middle of
it," I said. Justin had a dark and penetrating mind.
I ransacked the kitchen cupboards. A product
called Goo-Off always came in very handy. And a good ball
of twine, and toothpicks, thumbtacks, a waterproofing
agent, bug and tar remover, needle-nose pliers, duct
tape. I felt relatively secure in my preparedness.
I called Darrell Panza. He told me I was woefully
behind schedule. The sun was setting. I called Katrina
Kazda and told her that I was woefully behind schedule.
She said, "That has come to be expected of you, but it
is no excuse." I went into the bathroom and polished
the scales. I blew my nose. I looked into the mirror.
"You're the weak link in the team," I said. "You're
a disappointment to everyone." Then I went into the
living room and turned on the television. A newsman
said, "There are still no leads on this killer in this
brutal crime." I turned it off with a shudder. I
looked under the cushions on the couch—sixty cents,
a comb, a pen, two ticket stubs to a Broadway musical.
I have never been to a Broadway musical. I placed a
call to Marshall Aronstam. He said to not move. He

was sending over the whole team immediately. I said, "But, Marshall, I'm sleepy. Don't you think this could wait until morning?" "At your own risk," he said. "But I'm not responsible, old boy." We said goodnight. I called Felissa DuBois to say goodnight. She asked me if I had completed my tasks. I said, "Oh, Felissa, I'm afraid I'm far from perfect. I just do what I can. There are things I can't explain, but I don't think anyone's out to hurt us, do you?" "Things fall out of dreams, and sometimes the wind blows them around, and you find pieces of other people's dreams right in your own house," she said. "I found a medal commemorating the launching of the USS Enterprise in my bed this morning. It's so beautiful, but don't tell anyone, Joshua." "My lips are sealed. Goodnight, Felissa," I said.

The Rally

There was some kind of rally going on in the
common. Somebody was speaking into a bullhorn to
about three hundred people, who were cheering and
shouting things. I decided to drift over and check
it out. The speaker was saying, "Even my three-year-
old son knows better than to kick a goat." I mingled
with the crowd. A woman yelled, "You got a great big
cherry pie on your head!" And a dozen others said,
"Yes you do." The man continued, "And, then, the dog
ate our sofa. Did we kick it? No we didn't." Someone
shouted, "The saints dropped the ball on that one."
The man said, "I been down there where even the little
birdies fear to roam. I once found an angry viper
in my pocket, but I steered the course. I bonged myself
with a hidden cloud." "And you never lost your way,"
many shrieked. I was working my way toward the front.
The excitement was catching. "If you spit in a burning
skillet, sure, it sizzles, and then it's gone, and what
have you got? You have the memory of the sizzle, but,
soon that, too, is gone, and you're poorer than you were
before," he said. "Your duck just sat on a firecracker,"
I cheered. The speaker stopped and tried to locate
the man who had spoken those words. The crowd, too,
was looking around. I acted as though I were looking
also. After a considerable pause, he continued, "Never
before have we witnessed hairy hands with long fingernails
curl around the puffballs of history with such miraculous
dexterity." The people went crazy. They started bumping
one another's foreheads. I was bumping, and getting
bumped. "It was no accident I swallowed an ant this
morning while preparing my remarks for this rally. I
wanted to swallow that ant," he said. People had stopped
bumping, and now many of them were wiping away tears.
I had to admit, he was a powerful speaker. "And now we
are on the verge of setting sail the little headache and
the big headache, too, and we can see the fireflies, who
had all but forgotten us, beating their wings like idiot

children coming back from a dull day in the park, and
it is beautiful, can't you see just how marvelous it is?"
he said. "We love the idiot children," someone shouted.
"Fireflies can't drive tractors," another yelled. "What
happened to the pig?" I said. The man next to me looked
disgusted. "There is no pig," he said.

The Case of Aaron Novak

When I got home, there was a message on my answering
machine that said, "Aaron Novak, you're a dead man, do you
hear me? A dead man." The man sounded like he meant it.
Lucky for me, I'm not Aaron Novak, nor do I know anyone
by that name. I called the police. They sent someone
out right away, an Officer Rotello. He listened
to the message several times. "Are you sure you're not
Aaron Novak?" he asked for the second time. "My name is
Owen Nolan," I said. "Well, that sounds an awful lot like
Aaron Novak to me," he said. "It could be just an honest
mistake." "But this man wants to kill Aaron Novak. Aren't
you going to do anything about that? You could check in
the phone book for an Aaron Novak, and call him," I said.
"That's brilliant," he said. "Then I could pay him a visit,
and see if we could get to the heart of this." He shook
my hand and said, "You've been a lot of help, Mr. Novak."
I said, "Nolan." "You might want to take the tape from my
machine, I mean, for analyzing purposes," I said. "Of course,"
he said, "I was just going to ask you about that. You're
awfully good. Did you ever consider a career in the force?"
"I think about it almost constantly," I said. Just then,
the phone rang. We both froze and stared at it. "You
answer it," I said. "But it's your phone," he said. "You'll
know how to handle him better," I insisted. Officer Rotello
picked up the phone on the fourth ring. "Hello," he said,
and then he listened for a while. He put his hand over
the receiver and whispered to me, "It's Aaron's mother. She
says she's baked you, I mean him, a pie, and wants to come
over right away. What should I say?" "Tell her you have
a date, and won't be home until late," I said. "Mother," he
said, "I have a date." Officer Rotello looked miserable
as he listened to her response. He put his hand over the
receiver. "She said that if it was with that strumpet Leda
McKenry she didn't want to ever see me, I mean him, again,"
he said. "What should I say?" "Tell her it's with a new
girl named Angela Swift, and you're sure she would really
like her," I said. Aaron's mother wouldn't let him off the

90

phone. She told him that he didn't love her, and he said,
"No, Ma, you mean everything to me, honest. I'd do anything
for you." And she said, "I'll just feed this pie to the birds
in the morning. The birds love me more than you ever did."
At some point, I grabbed the phone out of his hand and said,
"Fuck you, Mother. All you ever do is whimper and whine.
Why don't you go work in a soup kitchen and help someone
other than your pathetic self," and I slammed the phone down.
Officer Rotello looked up at me and a slow smile came across
his face. "That was amazing," he said. "I could have never
done that. I was going to let that bitch keep me on the phone
all night." "What are you going to do about Aaron Novak?" I
said. "For a while there, I thought I was Aaron Novak," he
said. "He could be in serious trouble," I said. "He probably
deserves it," he said. "Do you want some coffee?" I said.

The Rebel

I drove north about two hours, until I came to
a red barn with the word SURRENDER written on it in
white paint. Then, I took a right onto a gravel road
and stayed on it for a number of miles. At the fifth
crossroad, I took a left onto a narrow dirt road. It
was fairly washed out and gutted, so I minced along at
a snail's pace. Some milk cows took a mild interest in
me. A few horses and a donkey watched. Eventually, the
road stopped at the river. I got out and looked around.
It was a pretty spot. Behind some huge maple trees
there was a little shack. I walked over and knocked on
the door, then slid a twenty-dollar bill under it. The
door opened, but it was so dark in there I could barely
make out a human form. "Come in, come in," a whispering
voice said. "I remember you, you've been here before."
I had to stoop to get in the doorway. He was a short,
thin old man, couldn't have weighed more than eighty pounds.
"Mr. Spaggiari," I said, "I hope I'm not disturbing you."
"Nonsense," he said. "How am I even going to know if I'm
still alive if somebody doesn't disturb me from time to
time. It's been a year since I've seen another human
being, and I think that was you." I still couldn't really
see him, or anything else, for that matter. "You were
very generous to share your time with me," I said. "Would
you like a glass of sassafras?" he asked. "Oh yes, you
make particularly delicious sassafras," I said. He led
me to a chair, and I was relieved to sit down. When he
had seated himself across from me, I began. "Mr. Spaggiari,
last time I was here, after much questioning, you finally
admitted to me that you did, indeed, write several of
Albert Camus' novels, and possibly a book or two of his
essays. During this past year, I have done considerable
research, and it has led me to the conclusion, that, in
fact, you wrote all of Camus' books, and provided him with
all of his major ideas," I said. "Well, you see, I loved
Albert. He was the love of my life. I thought if I made
him famous, he would see how much he needed me. But he

just treated me like his puppet, you know, a pat on the head
when I brought him a new manuscript. He didn't even thank
me when he won the Nobel Prize. Then he had to go get himself
killed." "And now that he's been dead so many years, are
you angry that you let him publish the books you wrote?" I
said. "Oh, never. I never believed in any of that stuff.
I just wrote what I knew the intellectual snobs and misfits
of the day wanted to hear. If you want to know the truth,
the thing in my life that I'm proudest of is when I held up
the Société Generale Bank in Nice, France in 1976, and got
away with nine million dollars in cash, gold and jewelry,"
he said. "That was you?" I asked, incredulously. "That
was me," he said. We finished our sassafras in silence.
"I won't wait so long to come back next time," I said.
"It's never too late to pull one more caper," he said.
I shook his hand, but the rest of him was a blur in the
darkness. "It would be an honor to work with you, sir,"
I said.

The Harp

An angel was playing a harp outside of Antonio's
pizzeria. I was already late to meet Walter Culligan,
and he was the man who was going to make me rich within
ten years. Other people had stopped and were listening
to her. They all had these dreamy smiles on their faces.
The angel stroked the harp with her long, white arms as
if she were kneading their souls. She knew how good it
made them feel, and this brought her great pleasure, you
could tell. The music was like nothing I had ever heard
before. It rose and fell and swirled and zigzagged, always
with silence in its heart, and eternity stitched through
every note. I had to ask myself what she was doing here,
but, then, I didn't really need an answer. More and more
people had gathered. The astonishment of sudden joy kept
all lips sealed. The angel's arms were swimming wildly
over the strings. I couldn't think. I couldn't even
remember my own name, but I was happy, if that was the
right word, in a way I had never been before. Of course,
I was in love with her. I would have given anything to
be alone with her, just to hear her speak. The crowd had
spilled out into the street and was blocking traffic. A
mounted policeman rode up and was studying the situation,
but it seems he, too, was quickly entranced. Everyone
was in love with her—women, children, old men and young.
"She's mine," I shouted. "The hell she is, she's mine,"
someone yelled. And that's when the brawl broke out. I
started swinging at anyone within range. And I was getting
pounded left and right and from behind. The policeman
called for help, and started bopping the good citizens of
the town with his nightstick. In the midst of the chaos,
I remembered my name and my appointment with Walter Culligan
and my future wealth. Someone had broken my nose, and I
was bleeding. I was trying to push my way through the
free-for-all, when I saw that the angel had been knocked
to the sidewalk. She was bruised and crying. I knew I
had to save her. With a surge of strength, I threw people
aside, one after another, until, at last, I grabbed her

hand and pulled her up. "This happens every time," she said. "I guess I really should give it up, but I love playing that harp. And I love people. The music is meant to heal them, bring them peace. Look at you, you're bleeding." She had a deep, gravelly voice, like a barroom angel, not an angel angel. "Well, maybe it was more peace than we could stand," I said. The police had dispersed the crowd by now. The harp stood by itself undamaged. "My granddaddy gave me that harp," she said. "Ain't it beautiful." "It's like a golden ship of light," I said.

Kung Fu Dancing

I had gone to the movie by myself. The theater
was almost empty, six or seven people scattered about.
I made myself comfortable in the middle of the back row.
A kung fu movie was playing, which I had seen many times
before, *The Dragon Lady Returns*. The whole movie is like
a dream to me. I know every kick and thwack by heart. And
when it starts up on this particular night I fall into a
trance. I can't move and I can barely breathe. I have no
idea what is happening on the screen. However, when I close
my eyes, I can almost understand the Chinese being spoken
in its rapid-fire way. I think they are talking about me.
"He's a good boy, isn't he?" "Oh yes, he's a very good boy."
"We should give him a puppy dog for being such a good boy."
"Sorry, sir, but we ate all the puppy dogs." And soon I
am riding a paper dragon through the air, high among fluffy,
white clouds, and looking down on towering, rugged mountains
and their valleys flowing with streams. A flock of geese
pass us, and I can nearly reach out and touch them. They're
in a hurry. They're trying to meet a deadline. When I put
my arms around the neck of the dragon, he hisses fire, but
in a friendly way. Now he's on fire. We're starting to fall
slowly through the cold air. I don't seem to be afraid,
though surely I will die. Someone, or something, is pushing
my arm, trying to knock me off the dragon. "No," I say,
"this is the way it is supposed to be." But it keeps pushing
harder and harder. I'm about to fall, and I don't feel brave
at all. "Wake up," a voice said, "we're closing the theater."
I pulled myself up and opened my eyes. A janitor stood there
with a broom. I felt drowsy and disoriented. I didn't even
remember coming to the movies. "I'm sorry," I said. "Were
you hoping to spend the night in here? Got no place to go?"
he said. "No, no, I'm fine," I said. " 'Cause if you lack
a roof over your head, I might be able to help you out,"
he said. I looked him in the eyes. The pupils were glowing
red. I tried to stand, but I felt like I had been drugged.
"I'm just fine," I said, "it's just that my legs are a little
wobbly. But thanks for the offer." I took a couple of steps,

balancing myself on the backs of the seats. The janitor's
eyes were burning holes in me. "I've seen you here before,
lots of times, and you're always sleeping. You haven't got
a home of your own, do you?" he said. "I've got a fine home,"
I said. "Where is it?" he said. "I don't have to tell you,"
I said. "You're lying. You've got nothing but the clothes
on your back. You probably snuck into the theater without
paying. I could call the cops on you, you know?" he said.
He stood there with his broom blocking my way to the aisle.
"I just want to go home," I said. "My dragon burned up and
I fell a great distance to earth. I'm weak," I said. "You're
one of those insane people that they let out, aren't you?
That's what you are," he said. "Let me by, and I won t hurt
you," I said. His red eyes were searching my face. I felt
that he had the power to melt me, as if I were made of wax.
"You think you can hide in here, but I've caught you now,"
he said. "I guess you have. I'm just a poor, insane, homeless
man, and you've caught me now. Aren't you proud of yourself?"
I said. "I'm just lonesome that's all," he said, and he
started to cry. I stepped forward and hugged him. On the
drive home, I wondered where in the world I was.

It was late at night. Darlene and I were just
getting ready for bed when the police knocked on our
door. "Is everything all right?" one of the officers
asked me. "Why, yes, Officer. We came home from work,
made ourselves some dinner, then watched a little tele-
vision. And, now, we're getting ready for bed." "How
nice for you," Officer Sturges said. He was the tall one
with the pencil moustache. "What is that supposed to mean?"
I said. "Well, we're still on duty, and you're just getting
ready to cozy up," he said. "Do you mind if we have a
look around?" Officer Kimball said. "A look around?
What in the world for?" I said. "Any irregularities.
You'd be surprised at the things we find," he said.
"I assure you everything's quite in order. A look around
seems quite intrusive at this hour," I said. They were
shining these huge flashlights all around the kitchen
from where they stood. "By the way, what did you have
for dinner," Officer Sturges said. "Beef stew, but I don't
see what that has to do with anything," I said. "Carrots,
potatoes, onions, celery?" he asked. "I don't know. Yes,
all of that. Darlene made it. She's a great cook," I
said. "I bet she is," Officer Kimball said. "Several
people have mentioned her cooking to me." "Just let us
have a little look around," Officer Sturges said. "I'm
awfully tired, but come on in. I just hope it won't take
too long," I said, opening the door. "Just let me go tell
Darlene you're here so you don't scare her," I said. Darlene
had already crawled into bed. "I'm in my nightgown," she
said, "they can't come in here." "You've got yourself a
nice home," Kimball said. "A big television, a comfortable
sofa, nice rugs. You're doing okay, Delaney." "Why, thanks.
Yes, we're happy with what we've got. We've worked hard
for it, though," I said. "I don't suppose any of this stuff
is stolen, is it?" Sturges said. He was holding a fake Ming
vase in his hand. "I want to talk to my lawyer before I
answer any of your questions," I said. They looked at each
other and then back at me. "I was joking," I said. And

then they cracked up laughing. "Oh, I get it, police humor,"
Sturges said. And they laughed some more. Darlene came out
of the bedroom with her bathrobe on. "Sounds like you're
having some kind of party in here," she said. "Would you two
officers of the law like for me to heat up some beef stew
for you?" "That would be so kind of you, Mrs. Delaney," Kimball
said. And so they stayed on and had themselves a late-night
meal. It was our turn to feed them, whoever they really were.
As they said good-bye, they thanked us heartily, and assured us
that everything seemed to be in order. "Not really," I said.
And they froze. "Police humor," I said, and they laughed
and slapped their thighs. "Weren't they the nicest policemen
you've ever met," Darlene said. "There's no doubt we'll get
special protection now," I said. "From what?" she said.
"I don't know," I said. "Go to sleep."

The Cobbler's Assistant

The cobbler was looking at my shoes. "You won't
get more than another mile out of these," he said grimly.
"But I have at least two more miles to go," I said. "You'll
never make it in these," he said. There was a monkey in the
shop. "Is that your assistant?" I said. "No, he's my boss,"
the cobbler said. "He's from Poland, the old country." "A
Polish monkey, they're common as fleas around here," I said.
"Go on, walk your one mile, and then you'll be dead," he said.
"Two miles," I said, "I'm going two miles," I said. The monkey
leapt up and screeched into my face. "Of course I'd be happy
to sell you some secondhand shoes, shoes I have repaired,
but have never been picked up by their original owners, leaving
me to eat the cost of my own labor and materials, the scum.
Some of them are politicians and big shots, too, but I'm just
a little cobbler from Minsk, with six children and a wife to
feed. What do they care about me?" he said. "I wouldn't
walk a mile in their shoes," I said. "Sorry." "That's what
they all say. I should stop mentioning that 'politician' part,"
he said. "Well, I had better be going. I'll just take my
chances with these shoes the way they are," I said. "Good luck,"
he said, "you'll never make it." Then the monkey said something,
but I couldn't make it out. I started walking in what I hoped
was the right direction. I could feel the leather on the soles
of my shoes thinning. An indescribable sadness came over me.
I couldn't afford to get lost. I couldn't afford anything,
really. A boy of about twelve stopped me and asked if I had
a light for his cigarette. I started to cry, and he punched
me in the stomach. "You're a joke," he said, and ran away.
I sat down on a patch of grass and reviewed my case. Maybe
that was what the monkey had said, too, only he had said it
in Polish. I hadn't traveled very far, and, yet, my shoes
seemed different to me now. They were the shoes of a very
old and corrupt politician who was never coming back. I
quickly banished that thought for a better attitude. I stood
and brushed myself off and began walking, almost briskly.
I imagined myself a soldier, and for some cockamamie reason
this made me happy. I imagined that my shoes were new and

spit-shined. People stood to the side when they saw me coming. I hummed cadence. I was on a mission to save the world. I had forgotten where I was really going, so full of courage and zeal was I. My feet were bloody stumps as proof of the good cause. An old man screamed that I should be ashamed. A woman covered her eyes and ran.

The Special Guest

Down the chimney came old Saint Nick, which
was weird, because it was noon on a hot July day.
He was covered in soot. "Well, this is quite a
surprise," I said. "You should get that thing
cleaned," he said. "We weren't expecting you at
this time of year," I said. "You wouldn't happen
to have a beer, would you?" he said. "It's so hot
in this suit you wouldn't believe it." "Sure, I
can get you a beer," I said. When I returned, he
said, "Where the hell am I, anyway?" I told him,
and he looked confused. "Do you know what day it
is?" he said. I told him, and he looked bewildered.
He took a long slug of his beer. "I hate to admit
it, but I'm not really sure what year it is," he
said. I told him, and he thought about that for
a long time. "Can I have another beer?" he said.
When I returned, he said, "Why am I dressed like
this? It's hot out there." "You live in the North
Pole. You're only supposed to come down here
at Christmas," I said. "Oh," he said. "Mrs. Claus
died. I'm lonely up there. I want to live down
here, in a nice little house like this one." "Do
you have any money, some savings perhaps?" I said.
"I'm broke," he said. "I gave it all away, I
have nothing." "You could get a job," I said.
"I'm too old, and, besides, I don't know how to do
anything," he said. "We have a spare room, now
that the kids have gone," I said. "You could live
here and help out with odd jobs." He looked around.
"Could I have another beer?" he said. I got it
for him. "I just want to get out of these old
clothes, and shave this damned beard. It's too
hot," he said. He really did look miserable.
"Well, you can borrow my razor, and maybe we can
find you some summer clothes at Mr. Big's in the
mall," I said. "I'm just skin and bones," he said.
"There's no meat on me. I haven't eaten in months,

maybe years, I don't know," he said. "Well, then,
maybe some of my clothes might fit you," I said.
"I'd like that," he said. "I'd like to be able
to walk down the street without people making such
a fuss." After another beer, Nick shaved and tried
on one of my shirts and a pair of cotton slacks.
He was a gaunt, old man, who stayed in his room
most of the time. He seemed to not remember his
old life at the Pole, so Jill and I never mentioned
it. He liked to rake leaves in the fall, I don't
know why. Jill knitted him a sweater, and he cried
when she gave it to him. Then he kissed her, and
I said, "That's enough."

Faultfinding Tour

I was on a faultfinding tour of my own soul.
Oily rags everywhere, there's a nut missing there,
a hinge blowing in the wind, paint peeling, cracked
windowpane, water dripping, plugged drain, dust babies
twisting in the night. It's not so bad. It will still
fly. A few creaks and shudders. I recall a thousand
years ago I was fighting for my life. An angel in a
tree surprised me. A snake swallowed me, and I
traveled that way for years. It was dark and I was
thirsty. Then I woke, and I was in a city. I ran.
I climbed the side of a building. People shouted.
Shots were fired. I was at a party, drinking champagne.
It was somebody's birthday. Colby Phillips made a speech,
and the lights went out. Somebody kissed me. I was in
the mountains being tracked by wolves. The wind was
fierce. I couldn't see where I was going, but I trudged
on. I fell from a cliff. It felt like flying. Indeed,
I believed I was flying. I held my arms out, and the
drafts lifted me. The wolves were howling, for that is
what they do so well. Their dinner was sailing through
the air. The stars were out. A full moon lit up the
little towns below. I was going home. My heart gladdened.
Love and work. Work and love. And the loud sobbing
through the night. What to make of it? The study of
maps, the naming of plants, the endless railway tracks,
the hawks, the bikes, the walking sticks, the masks,
the postcards and paperclips and lipstick stains
and you're never coming back, the soufflé was a grand
success, his death came as no surprise, the telephone
is on fire, the toys scattered across the lawn, a frog
the size of a dog, the police car slowly spinning in
the rain, hello howdy, how's your tooth, who stole the
newspaper, I'm sorry, I forgot, I didn't see a thing,
there's a newt in the basement saying your name, she's

gone to the store for some nails, a drill, a wheelbarrow,
a rake and a rabbit. The soul's mansion is ancient, and
sadly needs repair. Throughout the huge, windy rooms
a song still lingers, faint murmur or hum, forever,
yesterday, or never again.

The Loon

A loon woke me this morning. It was like waking up
in another world. I had no idea what was expected of me.
I waited for instructions. Someone called and asked me
if I wanted a free trip to Florida. I said, "Sure. Can
I go today?" A man in a uniform picked me up in a limousine,
and the next thing I know I'm being chased by an alligator
across a parking lot. A crowd gathers and cheers me on.
Of course, none of this really happened. I'm still sleeping.
I don't want to go to work. I want to know what the loon is
saying. It sounds like ecstasy tinged with unfathomable
terror. One thing is certain: at least they are not speaking
of tax shelters. The phone rings. It's my boss. She says,
"Where are you?" I say, "I don't know. I don't recognize
my surroundings. I think I've been kidnapped. If they make
demands of you, don't give in. That's my professional advice."
Just then, the loon let out a tremendous looping, soaring,
swirling, quadruple whoop. "My god, are you alright?" my
boss said. "In case we do not meet again, I want you to know
that I've always loved you, Agnes," I said. "What?" she said.
"What are you saying?" "Good-bye, my darling. Try to remember me
as your ever loyal servant," I said. "Did you say you loved
me?" she said. I said, "Yes," and hung up. I tried
to go back to sleep, but the idea of being kidnapped had me
quite worked up. I looked in the mirror for signs of torture.
Every time the loon cried, I screamed and contorted my face
in agony. They were going to cut off my head and place it on
a stake. I overheard them talking. They seemed like very
reasonable men, even, one might say, likeable.

Duane and I were hiking along a mountain trail
when suddenly it forked. I said to Duane, "What do
we do now?" "Well, the one to the right goes to The
Blue Devil's Swingers' Club, and the one to the left
goes to The Little Chapel in the Woods," he said. "I
enjoy hiking," I said. "I didn't come up here to be saved
or seduced." "We can go around them," he said. "We can
head north to The Petting Zoo, and then cut around to
The Future Farmers of America Ice Skating rink, and down
the slope past the Basque cemetery and military grounds."
"I thought we were just taking a hike in the mountains,
get close to nature and all that, see some birds, maybe
a deer," I said. Duane said, "How long since you were
last up here?" I couldn't remember. A little later,
we passed a meadow where the Battle of Bull Run was being
reenacted. I cheered on The North, hopelessly. "That
was really depressing," I said to Duane. "It's just part
of life on the mountain," he said. Some of the rebels'
children threw stones at us, and we had to run for cover.
I was now full of anxiety over what might come next. A
deer did run past us, but it had something stenciled on
its side. "What did it say?" I asked Duane. "It said
VOTE FOR BRUNO, Bruno's our representative. He owns
the mountain," he said. "That's great. I'll be sure to
vote for him," I said. "Oh, Jack, don't be so sensitive.
You never come up here, and, for Chrissake, you don't even
know who Bruno is. The mountain gives a lot of people
pleasure. I don't mind it, I mean, you never know what
you'll run into. It's changing all the time. Last week
I was attacked by a samurai warrior. It was really fun,"
he said. I was feeling very old-fashioned, perhaps, even,
antediluvian. "You know what I like about you, Jack? You're
so damned antediluvian," Duane said. "I am not," I said.
"I don't go that far back." We passed a statue of Theodore
Roosevelt. It was well done, a good likeness, but, if you
stood too close to it—and I found this out the hard way—

his fists strike out at you lightning fast, and I went flying over the edge of the cliff, and I couldn't tell if I was really falling, or it was a simulated fall. Either way, it seemed appropriate to scream. People still scream, don't they?

Red Dirt

An archeological team from a nearby university
asked my permission to dig in my backyard, and I said
no. They promised to restore my lawn to its current
state when finished, and I said no. They said the
university hadn't the money to offer me recompense, but
they personally were willing to offer me five thousand
dollars for my trouble, and I said no. I didn't hear from
them after that. They never told me why my backyard held
such interest for them. And I didn't think to ask. I could
think about nothing else for months to come. Was there an
old Mayan city down there, or Incan, Etruscan, Viking?
It could be anything. I was sitting right on it. Some
nights it was almost too much to bear. I could hear the
screams of the sacrifices. I could see the jaguar god
stoically watching on his throne of gold. How was I supposed
to sleep? I couldn't tell anybody, and I couldn't call the
police. I didn't even want people coming to the house for
fear of the harm that might come to them. My friends thought
I had taken ill, and sent me baskets of fruit. And, I suppose,
I was sick in a way. I had lost my appetite, and had grown
weak. The endless beheadings and mutilations had made me
numb. I had become a servant to the jaguar god, one of
thousands, of course, but I did get to come close enough
to him to see the serene beauty of his eyes. How could I
have ever doubted his cause. At night, I slept with the
other servants in an immense dormitory. We were as peaceful
as seraphim. When the winds blow, fine, red dirt sneaks in
and covers the floor. I dream we are being buried in it,
each day a little more. We go about our many duties, but
the dirt is inching up on us. In its way, it is beautiful,
the waves it makes, like the whistling of time. No one
mentions it. It's best this way. A peasant girl smiled
at me; then, she was gone.

Lost Geese

When I saw the Girl Scouts walking down my driveway,
I went and hid in the closet until long after their knocking
subsided. I have an irrational fear of Girl Scouts, I don't
know what that's called. Otherwise, I think I'm pretty normal.
Sabrina called to tell me her goldfish had died. She was
actually sobbing. "How long had you had him?" I asked. "Just
a week, but, still, I loved him. Because of my mother's wretched
cat, I was never allowed to have a goldfish throughout my entire
childhood. And now this," she said. "Can't you just go out
and get another?" I said. She hung up on me. I guess it was
a pretty insensitive thing to say, but I was trying to be nice.
I knew Sabrina's mother, and, it's true, she loved Miffy more
than she loved Sabrina or anyone. That was one fat, ugly cat.
I was flipping through a catalogue of amazing gadgets, none of
which I need, all of which I want, when the phone rang again.
This time it was my old friend Joachim. He used to break wild horses,
then he hoboed for a while. I always had a special
place in my heart for Joachim, until he found his way into high
finance, and now he bores me to death, but I can't tell him.
He wanted to come over and watch a basketball game with me,
but I told him I was working late on a report. Joachim knows
that I am unemployed at the moment, but he was polite enough
to not say anything. If I know Sabrina at all, she will have
an elaborate funeral for her goldfish, which probably doesn't
have a name, complete with church music and flowers and candles.
She will agonize over whether or not she should invite me, and,
in the end, she won't. Good. I hate fish funerals. I read
an article in the paper about the disaffected youth of Tokyo
who take a certain new drug that makes them feel like they are
successful business executives. So, instead of getting into
all kinds of trouble, they stay up all night making deals. A
police spokesman says he approves of the drug, thinks it helps
build character. Crime is down. The kids wake up in the alleys
in the morning and don't know who they are. Perhaps that is
the drug for me. Something will work out for me. It always
does. I'm just like one of those lost geese I saw today, circling
and circling in the sky, no longer remembering the original plan.

But they find a pond somewhere, and it's pretty good, so they stay and call it home. What's so sad about that? Oh, sure, it's a break with tradition, and they barely know where they are, but they're happy in their way. They fly around every now and then just to show that they can, and then they crash back onto the pond, and glide around, looking proud. "What happened?" one of them says. "Shut up," says the other.

Jeannie had worked as a waitress at the Duck Pond
Cafe for the past eight years, and, during that time, she
had met some pretty strange characters. But, last week,
there was one who beat them all. He was a dead man. He
shuffled in and collapsed in a booth, barely able to hold
his head up. She brought him a glass of water and a menu.
He grasped the glass of water with both hands, and brought
it slowly to his parched lips. Half the water spilled down
his dirty, blue suit, but he didn't seem to mind. "My god,
that's good," he said in a thin, raspy voice. Jeannie poured
him another glass, which he drank immediately. Though his
eyes were almost vacant, he stared at Jeannie's with deep
gratitude. Then he studied the menu excitedly. "I'd like
a double cheeseburger and extra large fries." he said. She
handed the order to Dennis the cook, but said nothing to him
about the deceased customer. She went back and filled his
glass several times, and each time he thanked her and tried
to smile. When his food was finally ready, she delivered it
and he stared at it in awe. "Enjoy," she said, and he replied,
"Yes, yes, I certainly will." She went back to the counter
and watched him devour all of it in several minutes. When
she went to clear his table, he said, "I'd like more of the
same. Is that possible? Are there any rules against that?"
"Certainly not," she said. "Coming right up." She delivered
the order to Dennis, then waited on a family of five who had
just sat down. She was happy that they didn't have a view
of the dead man. After he had finished his second meal, she
asked him if he would care for some dessert. "Oh, yes, indeed,
that would be excellent," he said. He wanted a piece of
apple pie and three scoops of vanilla ice cream. His voice
was coming back to him, and there was even a little gleam in
his eyes. When she delivered his dessert, he thanked her
profusely, and reached out and touched her hand. She started
to freeze, but then caught herself, and grabbed his hand in
hers. "What's your name?" she said. He smiled at her. "Do
you mind if I eat?" he said. "Of course not. That was rude
of me," she said, and walked back to the counter. She delivered

the food to the family of five. They suddenly seemed very loud and annoying. She much preferred the company of the dead man who was so quiet and grateful. When he had finished his dessert, she brought him his check, which he stared at for a long time. He searched all his pockets to no avail. "That's okay," Jeannie said. "Don't worry about it." "I was so hungry, I never thought about the money. That was bad of me," he said. "No, no, it was an honor to have given you this food. You needed it. I could see," she said. "But do you have anywhere to go?" His face looked pained as he thought that over. "Everyone has a place to go. I'll find one. I don't know how, but, maybe, something will occur to me. I'll just keep walking. Someone might recognize me," he said. "You just needed to get your strength back," Jeannie said. He stood up. "I can't thank you enough," he said, and shook her hand. She stood at the window and watched him walk down the street, staring into people's faces as they passed. He was somebody's father or husband or something, but he might as well be invisible.

One night, after dinner, Amy announced to me that she
was pregnant. In our three years of marriage, we had never
even mentioned children, so, in my shock, I had to sort of
fake my response, until I could figure out how I really felt.
"That's so great, Amy," I said. "We're going to be parents.
You've made me the happiest man in the world." "It's kind of
a surprise, though, isn't it? I mean, it wasn't as though we were
trying," she said. "That's probably the best way, when you're
not trying. It proves that it was really meant to be," I said.
In the weeks that followed, I tried to picture us taking care
of a tiny baby. I could see a featherless, baby bird, squawking
hideously, and me, crawling toward it with an eyedropper, which,
soon, turned into a dagger. Amy was crouched on top of the
couch like a gargoyle, snarling and hissing. That's about as
far as I got trying to imagine us as parents. We didn't tell
anyone our good news. We didn't even talk about it. If Amy
was seeing a doctor, she didn't mention it to me. We were
sailing through some very unreal territory, and the baby was
the captain of our death ship. I watched baseball on TV all
the time, rooting and shouting like a madman, when, in fact,
I had no idea who was playing or what was going on. It was
just to clutter up the empty space in my life that the baby had
created. Amy sat there with me and, occasionally, shouted
something like "Kill those bastards!" Then, she'd glance at
me, almost coquettishly, and smile, hoping I might be a little
proud of her, which I was. She was swelling up with each passing
week. I thought of her belly as a piñata, and, one day, when
I was properly blindfolded, I would beat on it with a stick,
and out would come wonderful candies and fruits and gifts.
Amy should have worn the head of an elephant, and roared loudly
whenever she turned corners in the house. She was that large.
I began to worship her, and, at the same time, fear her. When-
ever I brought tea and cookies to her, I bowed, and she
accepted this gesture of obeisance without comment, as though
it were her due. She was the queen, and I, her humble servant.
I took great pride in the performance of my many duties. I did
everything but bathe her. That was an entirely separate operation

jobbed out to independent contractors. I think we both forgot that a baby had anything to do with any of this. There was so much to do as it was. I sewed enormous, bejeweled gowns for the lady. I baked all night. I cooked. I shopped for delicacies. I chauffeured her to important balls and waited by the side of the car for hours, counting the stars to keep myself awake. Not once did I feel sorry for myself, or question my devotion. And, then, one day she said to me, "Jason, I think it's coming." "What's coming?" I said. "The baby," she said. My mind went blank. I literally could not comprehend her words. Our recent life had been so grand, even though I was a mere servant. "But, your Czarina," I said, "there is no room is this house for a baby, and, besides, I have no time. My time is entirely devoted to satisfying your needs, which, if you will forgive my saying so, are many. A baby would break this poor camel's back."
"Be that as it may," she said, "the baby is coming." That night, I was filled with foreboding. I could hear the pounding hooves of the wild tribes of Genghis Khan coming over the mountains to rape and pillage our little kingdom, and I cried for mercy, but there was none. There was only the little baby from now on.

Conventional Medicine

When I was released from the hospital, no one was
waiting for me. The hospital was in a part of town I
barely knew. The streets were quiet, almost deserted.
I searched the horizon for a landmark without success.
I started walking down Primean Street with its sad, boarded-
up shops, tattoo parlor, pawn shop, fortune-teller, Last
Chance Full Gospel Assembly. I walked on. Soon, there
were little houses with children playing in the yards.
Then, the houses got bigger, and the shrubs were trimmed,
and there were fine cars in the driveways. Still,
I recognized nothing, and no one spoke to me. I thought, maybe I don't
live here. I climbed the steps to one of the mansions, and
rang the doorbell. I had no idea what I would say if some-
one answered. I rang it a second time. When no one answered,
I tried the doorknob. To my surprise, the door opened,
and I walked right in. "I'm home!" I shouted. It was quite
a grand house, a lovely, spiral staircase off to one side,
and a dining room fit for royalty. But, what's odd, is that
I instantly felt it was mine. I looked into the refrigerator,
and found some leftover roast chicken to satisfy my immediate
hunger. I poured myself a glass of iced tea and strolled
from room to room, impressed with my immaculate taste. The
family photos framed on the fireplace mantel brought back
many memories. I stood staring at them for a long time.
I was lost in reverie when I heard footsteps.
I didn't have time to panic before I was confronted by a child,
a boy of maybe seven or eight. "Who are you?" he said. "I'm
your father," I said. "No, you're not," he said. "Then, I'm
your uncle," I said. "No, you're not," he said. "Then, who
am I?" I said. "You're a thief," he said. "No, I'm not," I
said. "Then, you're a murderer," he said. "No, I'm not," I
said. "You don't look like a plumber or an electrician," he
said. "I'm neither," I said, "I just got out of the hospital,
and I'm lost." "That still doesn't explain your presence in
my house," he said. "What's your name?" I said. "My name's
Hunter," he said. "Well, actually, Hunter, I'm a detective,
and I'm investigating your father on some very serious charges,"

I said. "I hope you nail the bastard," he said. "I think we
have all the evidence we need to put him away for a long time,"
I said. "Good," Hunter said. "I'm going to go get some milk.
Would you like some?" "Thanks, but I've got some iced tea,"
I said. I rubbed my fingerprints off the front doorknob,
and quietly closed the door. The mansions were giving way to
more modest homes. Women were pushing baby carriages, and buses
chugged along the street. Old men on benches were reading
newspapers. I sat down beside one, and said, "I'm trying to
find Locust Avenue. Can you help me?" "You're on Locust Avenue.
Locust Avenue goes to the end of the world. Everything is Locust
Avenue if you live long enough. What are you, nuts or something?"
he said. "Of course," I said, "excuse me. I was just suffering
a moment of vertigo, hanging from bridges, jumping out of airplanes,
but I'm on my feet now, and I'm on my way, sorry to bother you."
I knew where I was now. I was almost home. I lived on a cliff
above the sea under a pile of crumbling stones. Ah, the beautiful
sea!

Every five minutes or so a police car drove by telling
us not to go out through its bullhorn. I said to Amelia,
"I'm dying to know what's out there." She said, "That's why
they're doing this, don't you think?" "It looks like it's
a beautiful day outside. I don't see any evil lurking out
there. Everything's in bloom, blue skies, lovely, white clouds,"
I said. "That's when they attack," she said. "Who?" I said.
"How the hell should I know," she said, "some kind of phantoms,
known only to the police, seen only by the police." "Well,
that's ridiculous. Why should I believe them. Now, if they'd
tell us that there was a mountain lion loose in the neighborhood,
that would be something I could understand and respect," I said.
"I'm going to walk to town." Amelia didn't try to stop me.
"I'll expect you home by dinner," was all she said. Every time
I heard a police car coming I hid behind a tree or a bush. No
one else was out driving or walking or working in their yards.
It made me sad to think I lived in a town with a bunch of cowards.
The birds were singing, though, and this got me to whistling
a happy tune. The ducking and hiding got to be a game I didn't
mind. I assumed I would be punished if caught, but the police
weren't monsters. They weren't going to cut off my little finger
or anything like that. They weren't going to blind me. They
were just afraid of things I couldn't see. I was crossing the
bridge over the little creek when I heard another squad car
coming. There was no place to hide, so I instinctively jumped over
the rail into the water. The water's not very deep, and I twisted
my ankle on some rocks. I crouched in the cold water until the
car had passed. My ankle hurt like hell. I curled up on the
bank of the creek under the bridge, and felt like crying. I
could hear another squad car coming, blaring its fearful message.
I was afraid of what I might do next. I tried to wash the mud
from my face. I dragged myself from under the bridge and looked
up and down the road. I pulled myself up the embankment, trying
to not think about the shooting pain. Suddenly, the street looked
like a place where anything might happen, and I had the power to
make it happen. I started to panic, but I didn't know which way
to run. I felt like an escaped prisoner with no memory of home,

and only a murderous instinct to survive. They were closing
in on me. I could hear the dogs. I dove under a spirea bush in
somebody's front lawn. "It's all clear now. You can come out,"
the car said. A few moments later, the owner of the house opened
his front door to let his dog out. The dog came straight over
to me and started sniffing. The owner walked over and looked at
me. "What the hell are you doing there?" he said. "The phantom
bit me on the ankle," I said. "It's nothing. I'll be all right."
"What'd it look like?" he said. "That's the thing about a phantom,
you can't see it. It doesn't look like anything. You're walking
along. It's a beautiful day, then, bam! it's got you," I said.
"You didn't listen to the police, did you?" he said. "How do you
know it hasn't already got them?" I said. He stared at me. "You're
on my property, you know?" he said. "I'll be leaving," I said.
"Beautiful day," he said. "You couldn't ask for a better one,"
I said.

The Aphid Farmers

I was reading this book about ants. If an ant is captured
while attacking another ant's colony, it is turned into a slave
for the warrior ant that captured it. And it will spend the rest
of its life attending to every need of that warrior ant, while
the warrior ant itself grows fatter and weaker and, eventually,
completely helpless, until it dies prematurely. And, ants have
cattle farms, well, the equivalent, only, in their case, the cattle
are aphids. The ants take them to pasture, and milk them, and
provide them with clean sleeping quarters. Some ants only work
on ventilation. The builders are constantly expanding the colony
to make room for the new generation. And the queen, with her set
of wings, which she only uses once in her long lifetime, pumping
out her eggs, cared for by her devoted retinue of servants. There's
something so heartbreaking about it all. Herding the aphids back
from the pasture before sunset, and then milking them, Oh for the
life of the dairy farmer! I put the book down. Aphids give off
a sweet liquid called honeydew, which the ants like to lick off
their backs. A thunderstorm passed over while I was reading
all this. The sky was a very attractive, if sickly green. A
blackbird told a joke to another blackbird, and they both laughed,
even though it was a bad joke. The grass grows at night, while
we're sleeping, very sneaky grass. I was standing at the kitchen
doorway when a car pulled into my driveway. I wasn't expecting
anyone. It was the pest controller. He got out and started
spraying all around the house, something I had contracted for years
ago, and now I don't even remember why. He's gone in about two
minutes, vast civilizations laid to waste. I could see lightning
far off in the distance striking the hills. A male and female cardinal
jumped into the birdbath and splashed around. My phone
was ringing. I wasn't sure I wanted to answer it. I've had crank
calls, really crazy people whose thoughts scared me. But, then
again, I might have won a million dollars, and I would hate to
have missed out on that. I walked toward the phone and stared
at it. Then, it stopped ringing. It was about this time in the
afternoon that Jolene has her first cocktail, and that's when she
gets lonely and tries to call me. For a long time I tried to help,
but it's always the same story, her lost beauty, her fear of growing

old alone. Then, she fell down and broke her leg, and couldn't drive for a while. She had her liquor and groceries delivered, so that wasn't so bad. But, then, she fell in love with the delivery boy, and, after a few embarrassing scenes, he wouldn't deliver anymore, and, then, I helped her out for a couple of months, in spite of numerous awkward episodes. She really didn't have anyone else, so I had no choice. I walked outside to get away from my thoughts. The sun was struggling to come out just in time to start setting. Two squirrels were chasing one another around the juniper tree. The air felt fresh and clean, like you could build something that people might find a thousand years from now, and they would stare at it in wonder, and say, "This is it at last, this is the secret we've been waiting for."

The Visiting Scholar

A lot of people had reported seeing the fox downtown.
One lady swore it had trotted right past her on the sidewalk
with a green tennis ball in its mouth. The detail of the
tennis ball seemed to really annoy her. Someone else saw it
napping beside the flagpole outside the courthouse. Cars
screeched to a halt to let it cross the street. It was seen
standing in the doorways of restaurants. A lady claimed it
stood up and peeked into her baby carriage, and her baby tried
to touch it. Reports of its size and exact color varied a
great deal, but everyone agreed that there was a fox among us.
The newspaper offered a prize of five hundred dollars for the
best photo of him, so I started hanging around town with my
camera on the ready. I noticed a lot of people were carrying
their cameras, and looking up and down the streets nervously.
I saw the fox walk right through a whole crowd of these people,
and no one even noticed. I was so fascinated by this, I forgot
to take a picture. "Have you seen the fox today," one of them
asked me. "What fox?" I said. It seemed as though the more
public he went the more he blended in. I saw him once wearing
a pink feather boa, of which he seemed inordinately proud. And,
another time, he was carrying a take-out carton of Chinese food
in his mouth. The paper never did run a photo of him, and people
stopped carrying their cameras. I never went to town without
seeing him. Why me? I don't know, except that I thought about
little else. I saw him once in a straw hat and sunglasses, sitting
right outside the entrance to the bank. Customers came and went,
some nodding at one another, and even one nodding at him. The fox
nodded back in a gentlemanly way. And, then, one day I, too,
stopped seeing him. I knew he was still there. I sensed him
everywhere, but he was no longer visible. He had so thoroughly
infiltrated our ranks. More than once, when I found myself talking
to a stranger, I found myself studying their eyes, amused at my
own flights of imagination. And, when they speak, I check their
teeth. Then, one day, long after I had given up hope of ever seeing
him again, I spotted the fox in the alley beside the ice-cream shop.
I was with my friend Mitzi, and I pointed to him and told her to
look. He was mangy and thin, looked as if he was nearly starved

to death. "It's a huge rat!" she said. "No, it's the fox. Don't you remember him?" I said. "It's dangerous, it could kill us," she said. "It's sick," I said, "it's dying." The fox was crouching, and making a barely audible guttural sound. I started walking toward it. "Don't, Neil. It will bite you," Mitzi said. I held out my hand toward it. "Neil!" Mitzi shouted again. "It's a giant rat, and you will catch the plague." I put my hand on its head. Before my own eyes, it began to shrink, and then it disappeared, until I held only a few red hairs in my hand. "What was that?" Mitzi said. "I guess he went home," I said. "Is that far from here?" she said. "No," I said, "I think he lives in that apartment above the funeral home. I think he's writing a book."

The Reenactors

I was just standing on the corner watching the people
go by. Occasionally, an acquaintance would stop to make small
talk. "I'm just back from a year in China." "Oh, I didn't
realize you were gone." "My dog just gave birth to a litter
of eight puppies. Would you like one?" "Thanks, I'd like all
eight, but not today." "Hey, Blake, I saw you in the papers.
That was really a weird article. It's not true, is it?" "I'm
hardly the one to ask. I mean, it's my life, but who can say
what's really going on?" I must admit, I don't even know the
names of any of these people. But I know who they are. He's
the one who talks out loud to himself in bookstores. And that
one's unemployed. And that one's a scam artist. And that one
won a million dollars in a personal injury lawsuit. Then, a
motorcycle convoy roared through town, old men with a lot of
pride in their machines, on a Saturday outing. No one pays them
any attention, and soon they're gone. I saw my friend, Blaine,
crossing the street toward me. "You're just the man I wanted
to see," he said. "You won't believe what's going on. Some
out-of-town investors are planning to take over this whole town
and turn us into a theme park." "It could be fun," I said. "What's
the theme?" "I think they want to call it The Last Small Town
in America, or something like that, and everything is going to
be a replica, a fake hardware store, with a professional actor
reenacting the role of an old timer hardware store owner, etc. . . . .
The whole town reenacting small town America as it once ostensibly
was, according to the billionaire investors who have never even
seen an honest-to-god small town. We've got to stop them, Blake.
This is where we live. It isn't perfect, but at least it's real,"
he said. I had never seen Blaine quite so agitated. Normally,
he was a real cool customer. "Where did you hear about this?"
I said. "They're trying to buy up every business on Main Street.
They're offering the owners prices they can't refuse. It's going
to happen before you know it," he said. "Well, I'm not moving,"
I said, "and I can't change. I'll still be standing right here."
"But people will be taking pictures of you, and talking about you
right to your face, as though you weren't an actual human being,"
he said. "Sounds like a mighty poor theme park, if you ask me.

Are you telling me that people are going to travel halfway around the world and pay money to see me standing on a street corner?" I said. He paused and looked me over. "Listen, I have to run now. I just thought you should be the first to know, Blake. I know you love this town as much as I do. Hey, I'll call you when I know more," he said, and took off running down the street. Nothing ever changes in this town. One restaurant closes, and another opens up, and they're pretty much the same. Fears come in all colors, as they always have, and dreams, too. You stand on the corner long enough, and it all goes by. But I don't need to see it all, just a glimpse of Blaine on the run. Tomorrow he won't remember a thing. We'll reenact our lives as if they were the real thing.

We had a band for a while called The Evil Twin. It was
me and Eddie and Johnny and Parker and a guy called Android
from Tylersville. We were pretty good. Eddie and I had a little
house where we practiced, and Johnny had the van for traveling
to our gigs. Android played drums, and he was a little scary.
In fact, he was awesome, and he was sure we were going to be
world famous some day, the sooner the better. Johnny was our
lead singer, and he was good in his way, always working on his
moves, checking out the girls. Eddie and I wrote the songs.
I'd roll out of bed with a phrase on my mind and start searching
for the chords. He'd pick up his bass and join in. It was a work
of love. We had managed to record one CD with a very small label.
We had a party when it came out and invited all of our friends,
and everybody who'd been supportive of us. And, naturally, we
were playing the CD and whooping it up and yelling along with it.
It sounded really good. But when the fifth song came on, "You
Misty-eyed Devil," something strange happened, was happening.
There was a girl's voice right behind Johnny's, and was, like,
from another world. A high, soft soprano voice that twirled
around his, kind of making love to it, and disappearing into the
clouds. She was mesmerizing. We looked at the sound engineer,
Gordon, but he looked as bewildered as we did. "Who the hell is
that?" I said. "How should I know. She wasn't there when I mixed
it I can swear to that," he said. "She's amazing," Johnny said.
"We need her. I want to know her name, how we can get in touch
with her." The party went on, but we couldn't get her out of our
minds. Johnny was obsessed with her, and so was I. She was perfect.
She was just what we needed. And, of course, that was the song
that the radio started playing, not just locally, but all over the
country. We were traveling more than ever now. And whenever
we'd play that song, it was obvious that the crowds were waiting
for the girl to join Johnny onstage. Once, when we were being
interviewed by a big, national magazine, we were asked about her,
and I said, "She's Johnny's evil twin. We never know when she might
show up. She might be dead for all we know. She just comes back to
haunt Johnny whenever she feels like it." They loved that, and
it was repeated in many articles on us over the next year. Android

was thriving on our growing fame, and one night he asked that we place a voice mic by his drums. When Johnny started singing "Misty-eyed Devil," Android joined in a voice that was shockingly like the girl's, so feminine, so sexy, who could have ever believed it. The audience went crazy. After the concert, we questioned him about it. He said, "I just suspected she had moved into me, I could feel her there, wanting to sing. So I took a chance." "Is she still there?" I said. "I don't know," he said. Eddie was skeptical about it all. He hated the mystique that was beginning to surround the band. There was too much talk about the girl. "There is no fucking girl in this band. Look at us. Do you see a girl? There is no girl," he said. I had to agree with him, but then there was this problem, this thing we couldn't control, which was at least partially working in our favor. We cut a new CD, and she showed up on three songs, more beautiful than ever, and it was a big hit. Android kept the voice mic near him, and now and then she would show up and sing through him. He always knew when she was there. The audiences loved us, even when she wasn't there. But it was clear that she was the star, a temperamental, unreliable one, never seen, known by no one, perhaps even dead, unimaginably beautiful twin.

Johncy wanted to keep going. "But I'm tired," I
said. "My feet hurt." "Just one more hour. Come on, you
can do it. Think about something else. Pretend you're
walking on clouds, just bouncing along, light as air," he
said. "Thanks for the tip, but what do I do about my blisters,"
I said. "You're such a whiner. Come on. We'll make camp
in an hour. You'll be okay," he said. And so we trudged on.
I was sweating and panting and covered with insect bites. This
wasn't my idea of a good time, but I had let Johncy talk me
into it, because he's such a good talker, and also he's a good
friend. We had been hiking since 7 a.m. Finally we stopped,
and it felt good to take off my backpack and sleeping bag.
Johncy started gathering wood for a fire, while I put up the
tent and got our dinner things together. When I didn't see
Johncy for a while, I started to worry. I called his name
several times and got no response. I thought maybe he was playing
some kind of joke on me. And then it started getting dark. I
had no fire, so I started to build one in a hurry. And then
didn't know what to do. Should I eat without him, and just
go on as though he had never existed, get a good night's rest
and start out in the morning? For one thing, I could never find
my way. I couldn't go around looking for him in the dark, so I
just continued to shout his name from time to time. I made my
dinner, some pork and beans, some bread and a candy bar. It
felt worse than creepy being there alone, and I was worried sick
about Johncy, and hated thinking of the various things that might
have happened to him. I waited and waited, but still no sign,
not a whimper. I got into my sleeping bag and just lay there,
listening to the forest sounds. A hoot owl kept me company most
of the night. I must have dozed off toward morning, because,
when I awoke, there was Johncy sitting by the coals of the fire,
smiling. "Did you have a good sleep?" he said. "As a matter of
fact, I barely slept at all. Where the hell have you been?" I
said. "I did some reconnaissance," he said. "All night?" I said.
"I had my flashlight. This is an army training ground. There are
troops right over that hill," he said. "But I thought you said
you knew the way. You said it was the most beautiful lake you

have ever seen, the most peaceful. You said the Indians had thought
it was a holy lake, and that miracles happened there," I said.
"Things change," he said, "I guess." He wasn't smiling anymore.
I wasn't even sure he was Johncy. He looked scared, or mean.
"We'd better get out of here," he said. "I'm surprised they haven't
shot us yet." I took down the tent and packed it up. We poured
water on the embers and tried to erase our presence as best we
could. We trotted for a while until I was out of breath. Johncy
had stopped and was looking around. "What is it?" I said. "The
troops are coming," he said. "What are we supposed to do?" I
said. "Well, you can either run or be killed. And you better
zigzag among the trees as best you can to make them at least get
off a good shot," he said. So we started running in and out of
the trees. Pretty soon I thought I heard some distant gunfire, but
then I realized it was just a bird of some kind. I had no idea
where we were or which direction we were going. Johncy moved
like a deer through the forest, while I crashed and bumped and could
barely drag my legs on. I heard one shot fired, and Johncy crumbled
and fell. I stopped and knelt over him. A soldier appeared behind me
and said, "He was a fast one. It was just a lucky shot. I guess
today's my lucky day. My name's Rodney. What's yours?"

I was standing outside the courthouse smoking a cigarette.
A woman with a Scottie on a leash walked by and didn't even look
at me. When the Scottie tried to sniff my shoes, she gave it
a firm yank. A long, black car stopped to let her cross the
street. The driver looked at me and smiled. I gave him a weak,
forced smile back, because I didn't know what he was smiling about.
Was it that Scotties are inherently funny, or that woman in
particular? Anyway, I pretended to share his mirth. Then he laid
a little rubber and was gone. On the other side of the street, the
lady tied her little dog to a tree and went into a dress shop.
Everyone who passed the dog stopped and stared at it, and most bent
down to pet it. The dog accepted this indiscriminate affection
with good nature, and at least tolerance, until another dog came
along on a leash, and then it grew fierce, barking and struggling
to get loose. The little Scottie was pure muscle with jaws of
steel, ready to engage with a dog five times its size. Of course,
when a Doberman pinscher did stop to sniff it, it rolled up into a ball
and whimpered. All in all, it was a very sensible dog. The woman
came out of the shop wearing a different hat. She turned to admire
herself in it, then started to walk away. The dog let out
a quick bark, and she returned to retrieve it. She bent down to
hug it and perhaps give it a kiss. I crossed the street and walked
behind them. I wasn't following them, I was just going in their
direction. She tied the dog up again and went into another shop.
I stopped and played with the dog. A man stopped and said, "I once
had a Scottie. That dog saved my life," and he started to cry.
"They're the best," I said. "This one was born in a manger in a
milk barn. You could hold it in one hand, and the cows worshipped
it." "Oh my God," he said, "this could be the Second Coming," and
he rushed off sobbing down the street. The woman came out of the
shop and I stood up and said, "A Scottie once saved my life."
"That's nice," she said, untying her dog and walking on. I ran
to catch up with her. "Don't you want to know how?" I blurted.
"Not really," she said. "Okay," I said, "then I won't tell you
even if you beg me. But it involved a cobra and a sinking boat
and a one-legged man with a sword." She stopped and looked at
me. "I've heard this story a thousand times," she said, jerking

the dog away from my shoe. She was one cold woman. I watched
her walk away. The dog was interested in everyone and everything.
It was receiving signals, bits of information implanted and
transmitting codes only it could decipher. She kept jerking it
this way and that, denying it access to the bigger picture, so
that only fragments came through, making it crazy with frustration.
The dog's ears and tail were on high alert as its nose mopped the
ground for clues, but, thanks to her, it was all a jumble. She
forbade it to know the secrets that were hidden all around. I watched
them disappear into a crowd at the end of the street. Then I ran
after them. I found the Scottie tied up outside the post office.
I stood there, not kneeling, beside him. When she came out, I
said, "I could teach your Scottie to talk in no time." "You're
pathetic," she said. "Don't you want to know what he knows?" I
said. "I already know," she said. "He knows hamburger, he knows
beef stew. Now would you please leave me alone." "You'll always
be alone," I said. "I feel sorry for you. Have a nice day." I
turned to walk away. "The Messiah is once again denied," she or
somebody mumbled. I turned around. They were gone. "Code to
the universe," somebody said. People were walking past me. I
started back to the courthouse. "My old shoes," I said, "my old
shoes."

The Radish

I was holding this really exemplary radish in my hand.
I was admiring its shape and size and color. I was imagining
its zesty, biting taste. And when I listened, I even thought
I could hear it singing. It was unlike anything I had ever
heard, perhaps an Oriental woman from a remote mountain village
singing to her rabbit. She's hiding in a cave, and night has
fallen. Her parents had decided to sell her to the evil prince.
And he and his thousand soldiers were searching for her everywhere.
She trembled in the cold and held the rabbit to her cheek. She
whispered the song in a high, thin voice, like a reed swaying
by itself on a bank above a river. The rabbit's large, brown ears
stood straight up, not wanting to miss a word. Then I dropped
the radish into my basket and moved on down the aisle. The store
was exceptionally crowded, due to the upcoming holiday. My cart
jostled with the others. Sometimes it pretended we were in a cock-
fight, a little cut here, some bleeding. Now the advantage is mine.
I jump up and spur the old lady, who's weak and ready to fall.
I spot a mushoom I really want. It's within reach. You could
search all day and never find a mushroom like that. I could smell
it sizzling in butter and garlic. I could taste it garnishing my
steak. Suddenly, my cart is rammed and I'm reeling for my balance.
I can't even see who the enemy is. Then I'm hit again and I'm
sprawling up against the potatoes. I've been separated from my
cart. I look around desperately. "Have you seen my cart?" I ask
a man dressed in lederhosen and an alpine hat. "I myself have
misplaced my mother's ashes. How could I know anything about your
cart?" he said. "I'm sorry to hear about your mother," I said.
"Was it sudden, or was it a long, slow, agonizing death, where
you considered killing her yourself just to put her out of her pain?"
"Is that your cart with the radish in it?" he said. "Oh, yes,
thank you, thank you a thousand times over, I can't thank you
enough," I said. "Schmuck," he said. The mushroom of my dreams,
of course, was long gone, and the others looked sickly, like they
were meant to kill you, so I forged on past the kohlrabi and
parsnips. I hesitated at the okra. A flood of fond memories
overcame me. I remembered Tanya and her tiny okra, so firm and
tasty, one Christmas long ago. There was a fire in the fireplace

and candlelight, music, and the crunch, crunch, crunch of the okra.
I have never been able to touch okra since that sacred day.
We were in the Klondike, or so it seemed to me then. Tanya had
a big dog, and it ate the roast, and we had a big laugh, but now
I don't think it's funny. I remember the smell of that roast,
as if it were cooking this very minute, and I can see Tanya
bending over to check on it. How did we ever get out of there
alive? And what happened to Tanya? I look around, peaches and
plums. I'm butted from behind. "Watch it," I say to no one in
particular. Eight eyes are glaring at me. "I'm moving," I say.
But I can't move. The rabbit says, "Tonight we will meet our
death, but it will be beautiful and we will be brave and not
afraid. You will sing to me and I will close my eyes and dream
of a garden where we will play under the starlight, and that's
where the story ends, with me munching a radish and you laughing."
"I can't move," I said.

Affliction

It was a Sunday afternoon, and I'd found an old, shaded
dirt road out in the country on which to stroll. The wildflowers
were in bloom and the butterflies at play, what more could
a man ask for? I'm not going to claim that I entertained
great thoughts because, frankly, they were not on my agenda.
From time to time a breeze tickled the leaves. The squirrels
engaged in their esoteric games, not even they understood.
A large tin basin was disintegrating by the side of the road,
abandoned there perhaps seventy years ago. A deer leapt across
the road in front of me, nearly flying. But, still, I walked
in a sweet dream, unperturbed. I must have walked for a couple
of hours when an old man appeared around a bend. He had a white
beard and a walking stick and his clothes were the worse for wear.
"Good afternoon," I said, "it's a great day." He looked at me
suspiciously. "Who are you and what do you want?" he said. "My
name's Arthur Fairhall, and I don't want anything more than a
little peace and exercise," I said. "Peace?" he said, "that's
a good one. All my life I've had nothing but affliction, hard-
ship, turmoil, vexation and pain, and it's all because of this
damned road. It's put a curse on me, and now you're walking down
it looking for peace. That's a good one. Well, go on, have your
walk. See if you're impervious to its damnation, see if I care
one holy hell." I was so caught off guard by his impassioned
speech I didn't know what to say. "I'm sorry you've had a rough
time, but I don't see how you can blame it on this road," I said.
"It's this road all right," he said. "Once you're on it you can
never leave it. I'll be seeing plenty of you from now on,
you just wait and see," he said, and walked on past me. I continued
on my way, filing him among the more interesting cranks I had met
in my days. I spotted a raccoon staring at me from the fork of
an oak tree. A squadron of dragonflies maneuvered over a stagnant
pond. I examined the different lichen growing on the boulders
at the edge of the road. The farther I walked the more enchanted
I became. I hadn't planned on giving the whole day over to this
promenade, but it seemed there was no turning back. I had forgotten
all the chores I was supposed to do back home. I had forgotten
my appointment with Barney. I saw a little cabin up on a hill to

the right of me, with a path leading up to it. I recognized it
as if from some deep memory. A chill came over me as I started
toward it. When I reached it, it was all there, the kitchen table,
red and white checkered tablecloth, the coffee cups in
their saucers, the green leather stuffed chair, the calendar with
the girl and the lamb. I opened the door and let myself in. A
happiness such as I had never known came over me. I was home at
last and I knew I would never leave again. I walked around
touching the walls, touching everything. I sat down in the green
chair and picked up a pipe from the table beside it. Everything
seemed perfectly right. The old man appeared in the doorway.
"Where the hell have you been? Hunting rabbits? Well, I hope you
got one. I'm hungry. Now make us some dinner while I wash up."
I didn't have a rabbit, and he was going to beat me with the strap
until I bled. It was such a sad story.

Bringing in the New Year

A colleague of mine, by the name of Harold Chance,
had a terrible accident at his own party on New Year's
Eve. He was carrying a large bowl of punch across his
living room when he slipped on a throw rug. He fell
backward, injuring his head, but then the bowl of punch
came down crashing into his face. Harold was unconscious
and bleeding profusely. His wife, Ashlie, had been flirting
with a neighbor in the kitchen, but when she heard the
commotion, she came running to his side, and promptly fainted.
An ambulance was called, and when it arrived, I volunteered
to go to the hospital with Harold, even though I secretly
detested him. Harold had large blades of crystal protruding
from his forehead, which, for a moment, I thought made him
look like Miss Liberty. One of the EMTs said he thought
he looked like a saint, but he couldn't remember
which one. Then I looked out the window and forgot about
Harold. We were going so fast nothing was familiar. There
were people on the streets, but they blurred into one another.
I couldn't tell if they were celebrating, or just lost souls.
"Is he going to live?" I asked one of the EMTs. "He may
have already ascended," he said. The drive seemed to take
forever. I saw the female EMT take a swig from a flask.
Then she smiled and offered it to me. It tasted like some
high-octane blood. I smiled back. Even Harold appeared to
be smiling. "Happy New Year," Carmen said to me. She had
a name tag on the tip of her breast. I think she expected me
to kiss her. "Look," I said, "it's as if he's wearing a
crown of ice." "It's a very common condition," she said.
"We see it all the time." "He's my first," I said. "Can
the doctors remove it?" I said. "Not even God can," she said.
I looked out the window. We were parked beside a river.
Fireworks lit up the sky.

This woman had stopped me in town and was telling me all about her grandchildren. She even showed me pictures of them. They were all very cute. Then she said, "You must come over to dinner some time. Harry would love to see you. You two always have so much to talk about. I promise to give you a call soon." Then she offered me her cheek to kiss and waved good-bye. She seemed like a very good-natured lady. I had never seen her before. I looked at my watch as though it would steer me back on course. A few steps this way, a few steps that way, and then suddenly I was headed back down the street. I ducked into the bookstore, and as I was attempting to browse among the new arrivals a man came up to me and said, "That was a fine thing you did. Yes, sir, you stood up to them. You drew the line. Enough is enough. The little people will only take so much, and you were our voice, our conscience speaking. I'm personally honored to meet you, and want to thank you." I looked at him and smiled and shook his hand warmly. He was waiting for me to speak to him, so I edged away a few steps at a time, picking up books, studying them, and then putting them down again. Soon, the well-meaning gentleman drifted away, in apparent awe of me. Outside, I saw Jesse, but he walked right past me. He brushed my shoulder and I spoke his name but he didn't see me. I hurried to catch up with him, and then he disappeared, and I looked in several stores and up and down the streets, because I really wanted to talk to him. I had some good news for him about our friend Glen. A woman grabbed me and said, "Is that you, Hayden? God, you look so different. What have you done to yourself?" It was Nina. "Nothing. I'm just the same as ever," I said. "No, you're not. Something's definitely very different. Maybe it's just your hair. No, your cheeks have sunk. Oh well, what the hell are you up to?" she said. "I'm shopping, I'm shopping for a gift for my nephew," I said. "How old is he?" she said. "He's five," I said. "Nice age," she said. "See you later." Just as she said that, I had the feeling that Jesse had passed me by going in the other direction. It was just a feeling, I didn't actually see him. There was just a whiff of him in the air. I wanted to tell him that Glen was okay. I went back and checked in a couple of stores.

A man started following me, trying to tell me his life story.

The CIA had faked his death in Guatemala. They had killed a man
who looked just like him, same fingerprints and everything, and now
he no longer existed. All his papers were invalid, and he was a
walking dead man without a country or a home. "What do you want
   from
me?" I stopped to say, looking him right in the face. He looked
like a walking dead man, a sad, beseeching one. "I want you to sign
my petition. It says that you've talked to me and that I'm alive,"
he said. I gladly signed his petition. He seemed to have hundreds
of signatures. I forgot to ask him how many he needed. It was
starting to get dark. The streetlights came on. I stopped and
turned and walked back to the dead guy. "How many signatures do
you need?" I asked. "A million," he said. "And what about the other
guy, your double in Guatemala?" I said. "Oh, he gets to come back
to life, too," he said. "Then it's worth it," I said, and walked
away.

A pair of cardinals were in the window box enjoying the seed
I had placed there the day before. I was walking through the room
in search of a paperclip when I caught sight of them out of the
corner of my eye. It had been snowing for hours, and their sheer
brilliance was unexpected. I took a step toward the window, and they
    looked
up at me, and then went right on eating. It was as though I had never
seen a cardinal before. They must have ignited my incipient melan-
cholia, because, for the rest of the day, everything looked gray
compared to them. But in the back of my mind they were always there
reminding me of what was possible. I found the paperclip and returned
to my work, which involved several thousand pages on super-sensitive,
highly classified, transmogrified Jurassic and Cretaceous Trigonid
Bivalves Public Housing and the Threat of Modernity. I thought I
had a handle on it. Lord Fisher of Kilverstone said something about
urine and urinary sediment. He said Fear God and Dread Nought. But
what that had to do with urine, or the large cactus finch of the
Galápagos, or the parasitic weaverbirds, I wasn't sure, though he
was admiral of the fleet for a time. When I had to pee, I thought
of urine, but that's as far as I could get. Circumpolar arctic flora
funeral elegy and the mathematical theory of diffusion and reaction
in permeable catalysts sat in my lap much of the afternoon as I
watched the snow fall, hoping it would all be resolved soon, the pain
of it, the weight of it lifted, somebody would come along and haul
it all away. Toda Songs and the Athenian tribute lists and the
Khazarian Hebrew documents and the stranger within your gates, and
more urine and public housing and fits, passions and paroxysms until
I am weary and too weak to think any longer, but I am still shuffling
the papers, checking for pagination, for some kind of order. If it
is not perfect, I am only human, like urine in the housing projects,
full of sediment. Melanesian design and the wrath of Homer, the
decay of dialogue and the birds of the Ungava peninsula are swimming
through the voting districts of the Roman Republic blissfully unaware
of my longing to crawl under the covers and sleep. Why should they
care? It's none of their business. They are part of the grand design,
if that's what it really is. Some nights I have my doubts and I can't sleep.
What about the herbaceous angiosperms of the Lesser Antilles,

do they know about the plight of the Walloons, should I tell them?
Or is it all a sacred web of secrets, discrete destinies, a silence
like the bottom of the ocean where only a deep groan is heard from
time to time. I try to lift the mountain of papers. I can feel
spider wasps chewing on the Mayan hieroglyphs. They're hungry. Every
little bit is disappearing. Lord Fisher of Kilverstone is being
erased, even though he was admiral of the fleet. We won't be hearing
from him again. I'm standing, I'm walking. Add that to the trail of
miracles.

The Prehensile Tail

I turned on the local news. A baby was spotted crawling
up Interstate 91. Police had received over twenty calls
reporting the child, but were unable to find it when searching
the area. No one had called in and reported a lost child.
A truck driver said he had narrowly missed it, and nearly
wrecked his rig. A woman said she had passed over it before
she knew what it was. Everyone spoke of the child as "it,"
which I guess is okay. The police said they were still
searching for it, as was an ambulance unit and a dogcatcher.
I thought the child was surely dead by now, as night had fallen
and it was cold. Surely a parent would have noticed. The child
must have had a fine old time while it lasted, such dazzling
excitement, enough thrills to last a lifetime, at least a
very short one. I really admired the little sucker. Most
people are afraid of their own faces. I'm not saying they
shouldn't be. We're our own worst enemies, isn't that what
everyone is so fond of saying? But I digress. The child,
this baby, described by several of the motorists as being
approximately nine months of age, and wearing only a diaper,
was heading north on the southbound highway, and was said,
by some, to be laughing. Police cautioned motorists to travel
at reduced speeds, and to be on the lookout. There were other
stories, too, corrupt politicians, a shoot-out in a downtown
bar, a house burning down, the weather (not good), sports,
all ending with some inane jokes between the anchor persons.
I was just going to make dinner when my phone rang. It was
Daniela. "Did you hear that story about the baby crawling up
91?" she said. "Yes," I said. "It's awful. That baby's
probably dead by now." "I don't know," she said, "I don't
think that's an ordinary baby. That could be one of those
satanic babies. Nothing can destroy it. It could be on some
dreadful offensive." "Oh, Daniela, nothing could be further
from the truth, I'm sure. If anything, it could be the Messiah,
come to save our souls, and in his own purity and innocence,
he disregards the fatal dangers in his path." "Kevin, you
are such a Pollyanna. I should have known you'd come up with
something like that," she said. "But where are the parents?

That's what I want to know," I said. "Satanic babies have no parents, or, if they do, the parents are glad to get rid of them," she said. "Maybe the parents were murdered, or killed in a car wreck, and the baby escaped, and no one knows they had a baby, and the baby is just trying to find them, and now it's going to get killed because the police are too inept to find it. Daniela, we don't really know anything for sure. Maybe it wasn't even a baby. Maybe it was a possum," I said. "A satanic possum?" "No, our savior with a long, naked, prehensile tail," I said. The next day, the baby wasn't even mentioned on the news, and nothing in the papers, either. If it was headed for the north woods, I think it made it. In its own sweet time it will make its plans known.

The Reluctant Surrender of an
Important Piece of Evidence

I sat on the bench, waiting for Carson to get off
work. It was her birthday and we were going to go out to
dinner. I looked at my watch. My wrist was bare. I never
forgot my watch. Perhaps it had fallen off. Carson had
given me that watch. It was very special to me. I got up
and started walking around the park, retracing my footsteps.
I had stopped for a drink at the water fountain, so I did
that again, looking all around it. I had thrown a candy bar
wrapper into the trash barrel. I stopped and rooted around
in there for several minutes (I say that even though I had
lost all sense of time by then). I stopped and tried to re-
member where I had been before I entered the park. I crossed
the street and entered the pharmacy. I had to wait several
minutes before catching the attention of the pharmacist.
Finally, I said, "I was in here not long ago, and I seem to
have lost my watch. Has anyone, by chance, turned in a watch
to you, or have you, yourself, found one, because my wife gave
it to me, and I'm quite lost without it?" He looked at me sus-
piciously. "Anything like that I would turn over to the police
immediately," he said. "Well, have you turned a watch over to
the police, in the past fifteen minutes?" I said. He stopped
counting his pills and stared at me. "I don't even wear a watch,"
he said, "how would I know?" I didn't know what to say. I
wasn't even sure I had been in the pharmacy. "Thanks for your
help," I said, then, turned and knocked over a cardboard lady
holding a condom. "I'm sorry," I said. I looked up and down
the street. Nothing looked familiar. I started shuffling down
the street with my eyes scouring the sidewalk. A man stopped me
to show me a card trick. At the end of it, the queen of hearts
fell out of his ear. "You've got real talent," I said. I checked
his wrist for my watch. A sign said, L P D PIPE BENDING CO.
I tried to imagine what they could do for me, but I didn't even
own a pipe. I walked on. Another sign said, PSYCHIC READING
By Crystal. I wanted to meet Crystal. I thought she might know
something. There were beads over her door, and an enticing, far-

away music drew me toward her. I touched the beads and froze,
as though waking from a trance. Danger lurked everywhere.
"Don't be afraid," she said. I started to run. I saw an alley
and ducked in there. A mangy dog was chewing on a shoe. It looked
like one of my shoes. I checked my feet. I was missing a shoe.
"Nice doggy," I said, "now give me back my shoe." We wrestled
for a while, and finally I got my shoe back and put it on. It
didn't fit and it didn't match the other shoe, but I tied it up
and took off walking. The dog followed me, and kept trying to
bite the shoe. People were laughing at us. I was afraid somebody
would recognize the shoe and want it back, but almost everybody
had on two shoes, and they thought the dog was the funniest thing
in the world, especially when it latched on to the shoe and I
lifted it off the ground as I strode forward. Several times I
flipped it through the air, and this earned us a round of applause.
A small crowd was following us. The mangy mutt wanted his shoe
back. And, by all rights, it was his shoe. It was getting dark,
and people started drifting away. I stopped to give my feet a rest.
The dog was whining and whining, and staring up at me with his big
waif's eyes. "It's Carson's birthday, and I've lost the watch she
gave me," I said. I started running, retracing my way to the park.
My foot was bleeding, and the dog was yapping behind me. Carson
was sitting on a bench talking to an old man, who, I noticed, was
missing a shoe, the very shoe I was wearing. And I felt sure I
was in the presence of my watch.

Hilda Kupferman saw fit to invite me to her annual
party for interesting people. It sounded awful but to
her credit, at least, her definition of interesting did not
measure wealth or power, but simply people who had caught her
fancy during the past year. Of course, some people were
invited back year after year on the basis of something they had
done, or something that had happened to them, years ago. I, myself,
had been bitten by a wolf on a camping trip a while back, and
she never tired of asking me questions about the incident. There
was really only so much I had to say, so I had begun to embellish
it. "Under the wan moonlight, he tore at my arm's
flesh with the savagery of a god, but my free hand found a stone
and I pounded his skull with all my might. In no time the wolf
lay whimpering at my feet, my blood dripping from its fangs,"
I said. Hilda's eyes were popping out of her head with delight.
"Oh, Mr. Rowley, you are certainly a brave man. I am honored
that you have agreed to grace us with your presence tonight," she
said. The others gathered around her gave me an approving round
of applause. Of course, the story I had told was far from the
truth. Some wild furry animal, with a tongue like a dog's,
had licked my face as I slept on a mountain years ago. That's
all I really know. But I liked being invited to the party.
I was introduced to an elderly, aristocratic lady by the name of
Gertrude Falk. Mrs. Falk had been captured by a tribe of head-
hunters in Borneo while researching a certain rare orchid. She
wasn't violated in any way. On the contrary, it soon became
apparent that they believed her to be their queen, sent to them
from the stars. She stayed there ten years, until she had converted
them into the most peace-loving, gentlest people on earth. She
finished her story with tears in her eyes, and Hilda said, grabbing
Mrs. Falk's shoulders, "She's a saint." I spotted the bar and
a long table of canapés. As I was filling up my plate, a man
standing next to me was saying to himself, "Yes, sir. No, sir.
They are all dead, Captain, every last one." He was nibbling little
crab cakes nervously, glancing this way and that. He didn't even
see me standing right in front of him. He didn't look like he
was ready to tell his story, so I walked away, uncertain of what

to do with myself. A pretty woman stood alone by the door, staring down into her drink. I walked up to her, but didn't say anything. She didn't seem to mind my being there, so I just stayed. A man crawled by on his hands and knees, saying, "Water, water, all my riches for a cup of water." Hilda Kupferman was shrieking in laughter or horror somewhere on the far side of the room. The girl beside me finally lifted her head and said, "Do you believe in miracles?" "I suppose I do," I said, "I mean, almost everything is a miracle when you think about it." "That's what I figured you'd say," she said. The man from the bar walked by saying, "The reinforcements are not on their way, Captain. They were all slaughtered on the beach. I'm afraid it's just you and me, and the enemy surrounds us as far as the eye can see." "What about truth? Do you think there is such a thing, and can we ever know it?" she said. "You're kind of fresh," I said. "I don't even know your name." "That's what I mean," she said, "you can't know it. There's no way you'll ever know it. It's like a perfume, it's here, and then it's gone." "Oh well, it's nice to meet you, or not meet you," I said. "My name's Dan, and, once, on a mountain as I was sleeping under the moonlight, something licked my face, and it was a wolf or a mouse or a lamb, or maybe it was your perfume carrying your name on its nameless journey through time."

Polly tried to tell me that there was an underground
city beneath ours. "The people are very pale, but they can
see in the dark. Of course, there are no cars or anything
like that, but a few have carts pulled by albino donkeys.
They live on root vegetables, potatoes, carrots, radishes
and onions. Oh yes, and grubs, they love grubs. Their houses
are made of mud. They've never seen the sky, or light of
any kind, never seen a sunset, so they don't miss them. They
fall in love, much as we do. They experience joy and pain
and sorrow much the same," she said. "You really believe this,
don't you?" I said. "Oh yes, quite definitely, for you see,
Charles, I was born there and grew up there, and it was only
by accident that I escaped. I was blinded for several months,
and only slowly gained my sight back. 'Escaped' is really the
wrong word, because I never wanted to leave. I wasn't unhappy
in the least. I missed my family terribly," she said. I had
known Polly for years and she had never told me this story.
She was awfully pale, and her eyes were a milky gray-blue, but
an underground city was a bit much to take. She was a very
intelligent woman, an astute observer of politics, which was what
we usually talked about. So I let it pass. I changed the subject,
but Polly remained in a melancholy mood and was mostly silent.
A short time later I said good-bye. I promised to return next
Saturday for our weekly visit. I had tried to remain cool during
Polly's revelation, but once I had left I became deeply disturbed.
Either she was a complete lunatic, which she had successfully
disguised all these years, or she was having a sudden nervous
breakdown, or there was this city beneath ours with all these
pale people sitting down to a dinner of grub worms and radishes
in utter darkness. I couldn't get these thoughts off my mind
all week. There were times I wanted to believe her, even offer
to help her find a way back home. And other times when I just
worried about her sanity and well-being, and what, if anything,
I could do to help her. Saturday came, and I felt apprehensive
about the visit. I bought her a box of chocolates. She was seated
in the dark, and seemed particularly solemn. After a while, she
said, "My mother is dying. I must go home and be with her."

"I'm sorry," I said. I didn't question how she knew. "As you might guess, there are certain logistical problems. I have only the faintest memory of where I surfaced all those years ago. I was only a child at the time, and the shock of the light is all that has stayed with me," she said. "You must try to remember, anything, a church steeple, a farmhouse, a road, any- thing," I said. She put her hands over her eyes and tried to recapture when she emerged from the earth as a child. "I was completely blinded, by the light," she said. "You must see something," I said. "I can't," she said. "Wait. Yes, there is a church steeple, I can see it now, it's fuzzy, it's a blur, but it is definitely a church steeple, maybe fifty yards away," she said. And, so, we drove around. There were only seven steeples in the area. Polly was excited, and I was, too. At each church, Polly got out of the car and wandered around in fields, and sometimes people's yards. She looked like a dream out there, the wind plowing through her hair and lifting her white dress. She looked so happy. Then, when she had finally given up on the seventh, she started walking back to the car and something happened. It was late afternoon and the sun was in my eyes, so I didn't actually see it happen. All I know is, I never saw Polly again.

The Raven Speaks

I cut some roses from my garden, then went back in
and put them in a vase. I put the vase on the dining room
table and sat there staring at them for a while. They were
yellow verging on orange with a red border. It was as though
they were in motion, some private sea with tiny waves swirling
about. Several dolphins were leaping under a clear, blue sky.
I saw a man on a raft in the distance, just a speck really,
shouting something and waving a white flag, but then he was
gone. I went back to work, trying to solve some problems.
Three thousand units shipped there, six thousand over there,
nine thousand there, and so on and so on. I saw that it would
never be enough. Everybody needed their units. And the planet
was shrinking. You could feel it getting smaller and smaller.
I stood up and went back outside. The raven had its eye on me.
And I was watching it. It wanted to speak. It had something
to say. I took a few steps toward it. "Yew yew," it said.
"Me me?" I said. "What about me? I come in peace. I mean
you no harm. But enough about me. I hear you are afraid of
nothing. Tell me, is that true?" The bird just stared at me
and said, "Yew yew," again, and this time I took it to be in a
sort of accusatory manner. So I said, "All right, I confess,
it's me, I'm the one, I'm the source of all the problems. So
what do you want me to do about it? If it wasn't me, it would
be somebody else." And then the bird flew off, right in the
middle of my speech. I was just warming up. That was just my
opening volley. He'd made his point, though. It was me.
That bird didn't mince words. Perhaps he will return, and we
can talk again. I walked around the yard, always with the roses
in view. There's no way to explain what they do, or why they
do it. Well, breeding, of course, but that's just some madman
tinkering with the secrets of the universe. The roses, still,
have minds of their own. They're just humoring the madman.
Dried roses have been found in Egyptian tombs thousands of years
old. I think they know what they're doing, and it's beyond us
to even think about. But they're slowly revealing something,
that's all. Just shut up and don't ask too many questions.
A car pulled into my driveway. It was Dustin. "Sorry to bother

you like this, pal, but they need more units in Ethiopia, Addis Ababa, to be precise," he said. "Ethiopia?" I said. "I didn't know we did business there." "Oh yeah, big business. We're hot there. Can you do it right away. They need ten thousand units," he said. "I'll see what I can do," I said. "Sorry to ruin your day off, but in this business the clock never stops ticking, as they say. Hey, thanks, Skip. I got to run," he said. And, with that, he backed out of the driveway and sped down the road, narrowly missing a neighbor's dog. King Solomon and the Queen of Sheba want their units. The man on the raft is waving. He wants his units, too. So much pressure. The earth is trembling. The mystery brews in the soil, then pokes its way out and starts to open. We gasp, jump back, speechless, weak, fall to the ground, worshipping.

The Great Horned Owl Has Flown

I bought a stuffed owl at a tag sale, and immediately
regretted it. The man had said it was a great horned owl,
and his grandfather had shot it in the woods around here
maybe fifty or sixty years ago. He let me have it for three
dollars. I thought it was a bargain until I saw what it looked
like in the backseat. Even that dead, I thought it was going
to tear my head off. I waved good-bye and tore out of there
mindlessly, the fierce yellow and black eyes staring at me
in the mirror with an undisguised hatred. I waited for it
to spread its wings any moment, to flap and fill the car with
terror. I was driving erratically, too slow, then too fast,
not staying on my side of the road. Finally, I pulled over
and hid the owl under a blanket. When I got home, Sally said,
"Where's the milk?" "The milk," I said, "I forgot the milk."
"How could you forget the milk?" "I bought an owl instead,"
I said. I took the blanket off the owl and just stood there
trying to smile. She walked around examining it. After a while,
she announced, "He's very attractive. Let's put him on the
mantel. Now go get that milk." I placed the thing gently on
the mantel. It looked stern and imposing, as though it un-
questionably ruled this world. I couldn't believe Sally didn't
notice that. I went out and got the milk, cursing the tag sale
as I passed. When I got home, it wasn't there. Sally was in
the kitchen and as I handed her the milk, I said, "Where'd you
move the owl?" "I didn't move the owl," she said. "It's
right where you left it, on the mantel." She walked into the
living room, and said, "See." The owl was staring right at
me. Sally looked at me as though I was slightly addled. "Oh,"
I said, and she went back into the kitchen. Already it was
playing tricks on me. Then sit there like Mr. Innocent stuffed
bird. His powerful beak and claws were just a small part of
the problem. It was his mind that really alarmed me. He was
smarter than I was. One look at him would tell you that. He
was capable of operating on several levels of reality at once,
while I was barely holding on to one. I was definitely at a
disadvantage here. Sally called to me to come help her with
something in the kitchen. I looked at him and said, "You bastard."

I changed a lightbulb, and then grated some cheese. One thing
led to another, and soon I had forgotten all about the owl.
We had a pleasant dinner, during which we discussed the possibility
of remodeling the bathroom and getting a dog. Then we went
into the living room, and the owl had moved. "Why did you move
it?" Sally said. "I didn't, " I said. "It moved on its own."
"That's cute, Jay, that's real cute," she said. "It can do
anything it wants," I said. "It's not really dead. I mean, I
know it was shot and supposedly killed fifty or sixty years ago,
and it was stuffed and mounted, so you'd think it would be dead.
Maybe it's just us, but I saw its ears twitch and its eyes move."
"Jay, I can't believe you're talking like this. Are you sure
you feel all right?" she said. "It's had a long rest, and now
it's waking up," I said. I couldn't believe I was talking like
this either. Even so, I blamed it on the owl. "But I like it,"
she said. "Maybe it's the wisdom thing." "I'm going to release
it tomorrow," I said. "Release it? It's dead," she said. In
the morning, it was gone. No opened windows and doors, but
somehow it was gone. I said to Sally, "Did you see that, it's
gone, the owl's flown out on its own." "Yeah, it's flown into
the trash and on its way to the dump," she said. "The poor thing
was making you far too upset, no fault of its own."

The Nameless Ones

The moths come and eat everything within sight. They
come by the millions and darken the sky. You can hear their
jaws munching at night. It's an awful sound, and, in the morning,
the trees are bare, not a leaf anywhere. I closed the windows
and locked the doors, but still they get in. What they are
looking for, I don't know, a potted geranium. They're ravenous.
They won't leave until they are sure there is nothing left.
"There's nothing left," I tell them. And then they're gone.
They rev their engines, the sky darkens for a few moments,
and they're gone. The trees are bare, some of them will never
come back, but it's a bright day. I knocked on Connie's door.
"You can come out now, honey. They're all gone," I said. "Are
you sure?" she said. "I'm sure. Come on out and see for yourself,"
I said. She opened the door. She had one crawling in her hair,
but I didn't want to say anything. "My god, they ate everything.
I could hear them all night long. It was horrible," she said.
"I'm sure they must have gotten into the house." "Well, I've
found a few that I've taken care of," I said. "There shouldn't
be any more." Connie slowly poked about the house, investigating.
She found several in each cupboard, which I quickly disposed of,
but not before she could scream. "What the hell are they, anyway?"
she said. "That's the problem. Scientists have never seen any-
thing quite like them before. They don't know what they are.
They don't seem to be related to anything. They're as much in
the dark as we are," I said. "That's just great," she said. "Well,
at least they don't eat livestock and pets." "That's not exactly
true," I said. "What do you mean?" she said. "Well, there have
been some unconfirmed reports of missing cattle and sheep and
a few pets. And one child is missing, but you know how these
things are, a certain amount of hysteria has to be taken into
account. It will all probably work out," I said. "Whoever
heard of a flesh-eating moth?" she said. "It gives me the
creeps to even think about it." "Until it's confirmed it's
probably best to put it out of your mind," I said. "You know, I
hate to admit it, but they were kind of beautiful. They were
jet-black with those bright yellow spots on their wings. I almost
wish we had kept a couple to remember them by, you know, as pets

in jars or something," she said. I was shocked, at first, to hear
her say this, but the more I thought about it, the more I agreed
that it wouldn't be such a bad thing to have a couple of them
around, in captivity, as pets. I reached up and grabbed the one
out of her hair. "Ouch," I said, "it bit me." "Put it in something
quickly," she said. It continued to gnaw on my hand, but I found
a preserve jar and succeeded in getting it in there. My hand was
bleeding. I found a clean cloth and wrapped it around it. "Are
you all right?" she said. "Yes, but it was going to eat my hand,
that's for sure," I said. "Let's see if we can find another one,"
she said. I suggested we wear gloves this time, and Connie
agreed. We pulled out drawers and looked in closets and under
the bed with no success. "There's got to be another one somewhere,"
she said. But there wasn't. Connie finally gave up. She sat
staring at the moth in the jar all evening. "No one knows who you
are," she said, "and now I've got you. How does it feel to be so
alone, to be so beautiful, and have nothing?"

The Bus Stop

We were practically the only ones on the bus. It
was late at night when we boarded, and Nico snoozed on my
shoulder for the first few hours. There wasn't much to look
at, but still I couldn't take my eyes off the window. It
was desolate country with a few old shacks hanging on here
and there. Sometimes a dog would bark, but that was all.
The horses and cattle were sleeping. The driver looked in the
rearview mirror occasionally to see if he was missing out on
anything, but we didn't give him any satisfaction. When we
pulled into our first stop, Nico woke and said she was going
to get off and have a look around. I said I would join her.
It was a tiny town out in the middle of nowhere, but it was
surprising how many people were hanging around the bus station
at that hour of night, some really sleazy women who looked like
they aspired to be prostitutes, but they might as well have been
ballerinas for all this world cared. And the men who would
like to stick a knife in you for no apparent reason, except
the sight of blood excites them. And there were kids who seemed
like they belonged nowhere, so maybe the bus station was a kind
of home, and when a bus came in there was always a chance of a
miracle, against terrible odds. I waited for Nico outside the
restroom. When she came out she said, "Something died a very
painful death in there, or maybe it's still dying." Suddenly
I was aware of a man standing about two feet away, smiling at
me. He caught my eye and quickly introduced himself. "If it's
a dream house you're looking for, I'm your man. A little cottage
on a lake, perhaps." He was holding on to my hand and wouldn't
let go. "Our bus is leaving," I said. "Please let go of my
hand." "Don't be in such a hurry, my friend, until you've seen
what I can offer you," he said. He was hurting my hand. Nico
said, "I'm going to look for a policeman." The man had a
pencil-thin moustache and several gold teeth. "I am here to
help you, not hurt you," he said. I saw our bus driver boarding
the bus. Nico was nowhere in sight. "What about a car?" I said.
Another man stepped forward. "That would be my department,"
he said. "I can get you anything you want, at a discount rate,
of course." "This is sounding better all the time," I said.

"Just let me find my wife and we'll have a little talk about it."
The bus had closed its doors. The man with the gold teeth slowly
released my hand, and the two of them walked beside me as I searched
the small terminal for Nico. I soon found her seated on a bench
between two would-be prostitutes, who had painted her face with
eyeliner and lipstick and rouge and the three of them were laughing
over a bottle of brandy. "Nico," I said, "we're missing the bus."
She looked at me as if I were a stranger. "These are my friends,"
she said, smiling at the two bony women. The bus started pulling
out of the drive. I wanted to run after it, but I couldn't leave
Nico, and she didn't look like she was moving just then. "You'll
never find a finer place than this," the car salesman said. I
looked at my watch. It was three in the morning. "Even that bus
driver lives here, and he could live any place in the world.
When he's not working, he sits right here with us waiting for
the next bus. Everybody eventually comes through here, and not
many of them leave." "But I didn't see almost any houses driving
in," I said. "Where are they? Where do they live?" "That's
one of the beauties of this place. We've kept it real clean and
natural," the moustache said. I looked at Nico. She was nodding
out, her eyes all black and her mouth smeared red. We had to spend
the night somewhere, and this was beginning to feel like home.

The doctor's office was crowded, so I took the only
empty seat there was between a very large lady in a flowery
gown and a small nervous man in a gray suit. I felt that
they resented me for taking up their oxygen. Perhaps I was
imagining this tension between us, but I had no room to put
my arms. We kept bumping elbows, and I apologized each time.
Finally, the woman looked at me and said, "Are you contagious?"
I said, "What difference does it make? We're all sick, aren't
we? We're all going to die." She turned away in shock and
placed an embroidered handkerchief over her mouth. The little
man next to me stared straight ahead as if he had heard nothing.
I turned to him and said, "I suppose you're feeling all chipper
this morning? Nothing wrong with you, is there?" "Well, actually,
it's my bladder," he whispered to me. "Your bladder, is it," I
said too loudly, "peeing on everything, are we? That's an awful
mess. I doubt if there's anything the old doctor can do for
that. Just have to get used to it. Best not to go out. Lock
yourself up and pee all you want." He looked terribly embarrassed,
and I couldn't imagine why I had said all that. I was nervous,
but that was no excuse. I leaned over and whispered, "I'm
sure he'll have you fixed up in no time." The little man looked
up at me and said, "I'm sorry I trusted you. You're a bad man."
The big lady looked over and said, "That's right. You're a
bad man. You're supposed to be quiet in here, and stop touching
my elbow or I'll . . . I don't know what I'll do. I'll hit you
with my purse." A man across the room said, "I don't think I
like you either." A girl next to him said, "It's true, we're
all going to die. Let's have a moment of prayer together."
And she started to pray out loud. "Our Lord, who art in Heaven."
"Hey, wait a minute," I said, "we're all tense, we're all nervous.
We come here to good old Doctor Hautman, who we know has never
helped anyone. We should at least have a sense of humor. We
should love one another." They were all silent, staring at me.
The little man finally said, "I never have fun in the doctor's
waiting room. But this is sort of like a party where people
say all kinds of things. It's the silence that is really scary.
I think the doctors like it to be like that. It gives them more

power over us. We shouldn't allow them to have that." The man across the room said, "And they play that damned Muzak so that you'll think you're already dead." Just then, the nurse came out and called my name. I stood, shaking. The little man held his hand out to me and I took it. The lady stood and embraced me. "Don't go," someone said. "You can run for it," another said. I walked into the blinding light, we turned a corner, past many rooms, and turned again and again, until I could never find my way back on my own. She took my pulse and frowned. Then I sat there in the room alone for a long time staring at a chart of the human heart. I'd forgotten who I was or why I was here. When Dr. Hautman at last appeared in the doorway, I lost all hope of escaping. "You're a very special case," he said grimly. What made me special, he never said. The nurse led me back through the maze. The eyes in the waiting room watched me leave. It was as though they didn't recognize me. I walked under the sycamore trees, dissolving a little more with each step, in a light rain.

Macaroni

Tamara had gone to visit her sister for a few days and I
was on my own. I was cooking some macaroni and cheese and some
hot dogs when Jacob called. He wanted me to go to a lecture with
him by a novelist called Alexis Volborth, who had just published
a best seller called *War Is Good*. Jacob said it was a very funny
book. I thanked him for the invitation, but said that I had other
plans. Jacob sounded disappointed. I had nearly burnt the macaroni,
but still the dinner was delicious. I savored every bite. I had
even lit candles for the occasion. I had put on some favorite music.
Just as I was finishing up, the phone rang. It was a man calling
himself Wolfgang von Hagen. "Excuse me for bothering you, Mr. Metcalf,
but I heard that you were considering going to the lecture by Alexis
Volborth tonight. I thought you should know that Alexis Volborth is a
traitor of the worst sort, disloyal to his country and single-handedly
responsible for my brother's death. I advise you to stay away from
this most disgraced, most dishonorable of human beings," he said.
"Well, actually, I wasn't planning to go at all, but thanks for the
information," I said. I felt a little edgy as I washed my few dishes.
Why would he call me of all people? When I finished, I went into
the living room and picked up the paper. Another small child had
fallen down a well. Another dog had rescued someone from the flooding
river. The mayor said he had his hands tied. There was nothing he
could do. I put the paper down. The wind was blowing outside.
Branches were scraping the windows. Just then, the phone rang. I
was almost expecting the call. It was Alexis Volborth. He said
Wolfgang von Hagen was a liar, a thief and a murderer. "Do not believe
a word he has said about me. They are all lies, and, worse, if he
gets near you he will mutilate you beyond recognition. Trust me,
I know of what I speak. It is a pity you are not coming to my lecture,
because I would have made you laugh deeply to the bottom of your
    soul,"
he said. "Nevertheless, it is an honor to speak with you, sir," I
said, hoping to stay on his good side, at least. I lit my pipe
and took a couple of puffs. I must admit, I felt ever so slightly
important, caught in the crossfire, as they say. Without even
leaving my house, my opinions seemed to matter in this international
affair. But what did I really think? I guess I was inclined to

believe both of them. They had no reason to lie to me, a complete stranger. I lit my pipe and picked up the paper. The phone rang. It was Jacob. He said, "I'm calling you from the lecture hall. Can you come and pick me up right now. Something's gone terribly wrong. Alexis Volborth has been killed. And there are others, I don't know how many. It's mayhem down here. There are police everywhere."

"I'll be right there," I said. "But, Jacob, stay away from a man named Wolfgang." "Wolfgang's my only friend," he said.

The Coolest Thing

A long-haired man wearing only a loincloth came dragging
a heavy cross right down the middle of Main Street. People on
both sides of the street stopped and stared. They were speechless
at first, but, then, stranger to stranger, they began to share
their outrage. "That's a sacrilege," one of them said, and,
"It's just plain tacky if you ask me." The man carrying the cross
seemed to be really suffering. His bare feet and his hands were
bleeding. The cross must have weighed over a hundred pounds.
He was stooped and breathing heavily. "Take your bloody cross
and go home. You should be ashamed of yourself," someone yelled.
"We should just ignore him," an old woman said. "Where are the
police when you need them," a man with a red tie said. A boy of
ten ran out into the street and shoved the man from behind. He fell
forward and the cross pinned him to the ground. "That wasn't very
nice," someone muttered. The man lay there for a minute, and then
started squirming his way back up. He struggled with the cross
for few minutes and finally got it back on his shoulder and started
inching forward. "Well, he can't very well nail himself to that cross,"
a man in a panama hat said. "Maybe he's got a friend," a pretty
young woman said. "What's he trying to prove, anyway?" an old man
said. "He thinks he's the only righteous one, and the rest of us
are sinners," a woman holding a poodle said. The dog barked disapproval
of the spectacle. "Well, this is more than I can take," said an
old woman, and huffed away. The crowd was slowly dispersing. The
man with the cross had almost reached the center of town. Some kids
were throwing small stones at him. Mostly they missed. His knees
were bent, and he looked as if he might just regret this whole bright
idea of his. And if he had a friend, now would be a good time for
him to appear. But no one did appear. Even the kids were running
down the street away from him, chasing one another and screaming
something. A police car pulled up. The officer leaned out the window
and said, "You'll have to get that thing out of here. It's obstructing
traffic." "I'm trying to move it as fast as I can," the bleeding
man said. "Well, I'll have to arrest you if you're not gone from here
by the time I get back," he said, and sped off. The man dragged the
cross to the side of the road and put it down. He sat down on the curb
and buried his face in his hands. The cross started to smoke, slowly

at first. Then, suddenly, it burst into flames. The man opened
his eyes and jumped up, quivering. The cross was blazing. He backed
up onto the lawn of the new bank and watched it in awe as it was
quickly consuming itself. The kids returned and said, "Is that the
coolest thing you've ever seen, or what?" Motorists stopped to admire.
The man with the panama hat came by and said, "It's like a work of
art. It's a statement on our times. Of course I don't know what
that statement is, but I'm sure it has some sort of meaning." The
woman with the poodle said, "It's so beautiful I think I'm going
to cry." "I carry a clean handkerchief for just such occasions,"
the man said, offering it to her. "Why, thank you," she said, dabbing
her eyes. Several blocks away, one could hear the siren of the
fire truck just starting up, but it was almost too late as there were
only the traces of smoldering ash left by the side of the road.
The man and the woman had walked away together conversing on some
topic of mutual concern.

A Clean Hit

A bomb had exploded down the street. I got dressed and
walked down to see what had happened. The Whalen's house had
been flattened. But Hal and Rebecca were standing in the street,
apparently unscathed. Everyone in the neighborhood was pouring
out of their houses and into the streets. "What the hell happened?"
I said to Hal. "We were out in the garden, thank god, when this
plane flew over. The next thing I know, the house explodes to
smithereens," he said. "It must have been some kind of accident,"
I said. "Well, I voted for this president. They shouldn't be
targeting me," he said. "Friendly fire," I said. "What the hell's
that?" he said. "They mistook you for somebody else," I said.
"Well, they shouldn't be bombing in this neighborhood, I don't
care who they thought I was. Children and old people live here,
and dogs," he said. "I'm sure you'll be getting a letter of apology,
and maybe a new house," I said. "It's lucky I didn't have a heart
attack," Rebecca Whalen said. Joe Mizelle walked up. "That
sure was a clean hit. No collateral damage whatsoever," he said.
"How do you know they didn't mean to hit your house and just
accidentally hit mine?" Hal said. "Jesus, I hadn't thought of
that. But I haven't done anything wrong. I voted for him, even
though I think he's a shifty bastard," Joe said. "Everything we
had is gone," Rebecca said, whimpering into her tissue. "When it
cools down, we can sift through the wreckage," Hal said, comforting
her. "I'd be glad to lend a hand," I said. "Maybe your silverware
survived, if it didn't melt in the heat," Joe said. Other neighbors
had gathered around and were whispering amongst themselves. "This
is the price we pay for our protection." "Thank god we live in a
democracy." "I'm sure they knew what they were doing." "I'm going
to write to my congressman." Hal turned to me and said, "Maybe I
am guilty. Maybe I did do something to deserve this. It's hard to
remember, on a day-to-day basis, everything you've said and every
little thing you've done. I can be kind of a free spirit sometimes.
I probably brought this on myself. And someone filed a report on
me. Oh god, I don't want to think about it, it's awful." "Listen,
Hal, I still think it was a mistake. It happens all the time.
Those reports pass through so many hands, by the time they reach
the top somebody has gotten the address wrong," I said. "All the

photographs and all the precious mementos of the children that can never be replaced," Rebecca sobbed. "One of your boys works for the government, doesn't he?" Joe said. "He's just a clerk in Washington," Hal said. "Still, I wouldn't rule him out," Joe said. "You're beginning to irritate me," Hal said. The neighbors were drifting back to their own homes, their curiosities satisfied. Joe, too, turned and left, but not before adding, "I was just trying to interject a little humor. Sorry, no offense intended." Hal failed to dignify this with a reply. The three of us stood there staring at the smoldering rubble in silence. "Well, you're welcome to stay at my place," I said finally. Hal looked at me as if to measure my trust. Then he said, "This wasn't our real home. We have a secret home where we keep our valuables. Nobody knows its whereabouts, not even our children. There was nothing in there but junk. I figured they'd come sooner or later. And they didn't get the car, so we'll be fine. Rebecca, here, just had to put on a little show for the neighbors. You can't trust most of them, if you know what I mean." We shook hands and embraced. Then they got into their car and were gone forever. I memorized their license plate number—357 O19—for good luck.

There was a knock at the door. When I opened it, there
were two men in suits, both wore hats and sunglasses. They
introduced themselves as Officers Antliff and Merino and showed
their badges. "What can I do for you officers?" I said. "Can
you tell us where you were on the afternoon of the Kennedy
    assassination?"
Officer Merino said. "My god, that's forty years ago," I said.
"It's important that you try to remember," Officer Antliff said.
"I was just a student at the time," I said. "May we come in,"
Officer Merino said. "Oh yes, of course, please," I said, opening
the door wider and ushering them in. After they were comfortable,
I continued. "I was obsessed with a girl named Rosemary Goldberg.
She was my girlfriend, but I suspected I was about to lose her.
I started following her. She was under the power of a girl named
Carol. Carol could make her do anything, and that may have included
things of an amorous nature," I said. "And how does this relate to
the Kennedy assassination?" Antliff said. "Just be patient," I
said. "On this particular day I had followed Rosemary to Carol's
dormitory. Carol's room was on the third floor. I stood behind a
tree and watched them have a pillow fight. They thought that was
the funniest thing in the world. I felt like I had a dagger in my
heart. Rosemary never laughed like that with me anymore. Carol
treated me as though I were nothing. She never even talked to me.
Then they disappeared from view, and I just stood there like an idiot
for the next hour, my imagination torturing me. An hour later they
emerged from the building in matching white tennis outfits, swinging
their rackets and laughing. I followed them, darting from tree to
tree, sometimes hiding in alleyways. I knew how pathetic I was, but
I was out of control. There was nothing I could do about it." "Mr.
Wheeler, I must remind you we're here to ask you about the Kennedy
assassination," Merino said. "I'm getting to that," I said. "So
Rosemary and Carol had just arrived at the courts and were beginning
to bat the ball back and forth. Rosemary didn't even know how to
play tennis, but Carol had made them buy matching outfits. I was
sneaking past this little Cuban grocery store named Zagorin's where
I occasionally bought cigarettes or a soda when I heard a newscaster
on the radio shout the president's been shot!" "What was the name

of the grocery store?" Antliff said. "Zagorin's," I said. "Anyway,
I froze. Then I went inside and stood there with the owner, Perez
I think his name was, listening to the reports unfold, until finally,
the president was announced dead. The owner and I were both shaking
and crying. It was worse than if we had lost our closest friend."
"What happened after that?" Merino said. "Mr. Zagorin closed the
store. He handed me a lime soda and we sat there on a couple of crates
unable to speak," I said. "What about Rosemary and Carol? What were
they doing all this time?" Antliff said. "Well, I left the store
about an hour later, and when I looked over at the courts they were
still playing. They looked unbearably silly and irrelevant to anything
that mattered in this world. They couldn't stop laughing, and it
made me sick to my stomach," I said. "So that was it for you. The
president getting shot freed you from Rosemary," he said. "I guess
you could say that," I said, "though I never thought of it like that
before." "Then it was a good thing for you," Antliff said. "What
are you getting at?" I said. "And you were with Perez Zagorin, a
Cuban, comforting one another," he said. "That's right," I said.
"He was a good man," Merino said. "One of the best," Antliff said.
"What about Rosemary?" I said, suddenly curious. "Housewife, mother
of three on Long Island. Apparently strangled her husband in his
sleep, but nothing's been proven," Merino said. "Still quite a good-
looking babe, if you ask me," Antliff added.

The Investors

Von Hippel said, "Seeing all of you again brings such
joy to my heart. Life is a long journey full of misfortunes
and heartbreak whose greatest solace is friendship, and whether
one gains or loses a few million is really of no consequence.
I look at your faces today, faces I have known for many a year,
and tears come to my eyes. . . ." "Can we get down to business,"
Dampf said. "Here, here," Fishkin said. "My plane leaves at five,
so I suggest we get right to the point. I don't like this whole
Menotti affair. I think it stinks. That man is not to be trusted
if you ask me." "What about some lemonade?" Shick said. "And
perhaps some cookies. Who would like lemonade?" "Lemonade
and cookies sound good to me," von Hippel said. "Personally I
would like chocolate chip, but I will leave that up to the others."
"I think Menotti should be shot as an example to others who try
to mess with us," Dampf said. "His wife is very nice, and such a
good cook. Her manicotti is out of this world," Shick said. "I
would never do anything to make her mad at me." "Old friendships
are like old wine," von Hippel said. "I'll take care of it," Fishkin
said. "I'll consider it done," Dampf said. "What about Muckerman?"
"Muckerman's a nice man. He makes me laugh," said Shick. "He's
disappeared. He's off the radar. I haven't heard from him in two
weeks. I've sent some men to his house. Nothing, no wife, no kids,"
Fishkin said. "You guys really haven't changed in all these years,"
von Hippel said. "It's like you haven't aged, like we were kids."
"Let's take a vote on the lemonade and cookies," Shick said. "I
know a man who can find him if he's alive. He can find anybody
anywhere, I don't care if he's in Outer Mongolia, he can find him,"
Dampf said. "Then find him. He's got a lot to answer for," Fishkin
said. "Mind if I open a window? It's kind of stuffy in here,"
von Hippel said. "The windows don't open. Turn on the air-conditioner,"
Dampf said. "That's an excellent idea. I didn't know we had one,"
von Hippel said. "What about that Corngold fellow, Stanley, did he
work out?" Fishkin said. "He tried to double-cross me, the idiot.
I don't know who he thought he was dealing with. It was pathetic,"
Dampf said. "I can't get this thing to work," von Hippel said.
"I'll help you," Shick said. "Too bad. He seemed like a nice kid,"
Fishkin said. "Nice, maybe, but he had a greedy streak I guess,"

Dampf said. "His mother was sick. They needed money," Fishkin said.
"I didn't know about that. He should of just told me," Dampf said.
"He was just trying to help his mother," Fishkin said. "Jesus, knock
it off. You're just trying to make me feel bad. I'm sorry," Dampf
said. "Well, it's too late now. Of course, you could slip some
money into the mother's account. That wouldn't make up for the loss
of her son, but still," Fishkin said. "Enough already," Dampf said.
"I think it's broken," Shick said. "See, it wasn't just me. There
really was something wrong with it," von Hippel said. "There, it's
starting up. Can you feel it? It's nice and cool," Shick said.
"Oh, I'm such a klutz. I can't do anything. What's wrong with me?
All my life it's been like this," von Hippel said, wringing his eyes.
"You can call room service. That would be of great help," Shick
said. "I'm very bad at calling room service. I always get everything
wrong. You can't begin to imagine how wrong," von Hippel said.
"That's okay, I'll call," said Shick. "No one's calling room service.
You can't trust room service," Dampf said. "We just want some
lemonade and cookies," von Hippel said. "Oh let them have them.
I think lemonade and cookies sound good, " Fishkin said. "You're
trying to trick me," Dampf said, pulling out his gun. Von Hippel
grabbed him from behind and in one swift move he snapped his neck.
"Nice work!" Fishkin said. "That was beautiful," Shick said.
"I never did like him," von Hippel said. "Now let me try room service."

The Vacant Jungle

I sat there thinking, the minutes fall into hours and the
hours fall into days and the days fall into weeks and the weeks
into months and the months into years and the years into decades
and pretty soon it's all over for you. You slip out of the picture.
It is almost as though you were never there. Time keeps rolling on,
going nowhere. "What are you thinking?" Maya said. "Me? I wasn't
thinking anything," I said. "Yes, you were," she said. "I swear,
I wasn't thinking anything. My head's a blank. I had a long day,"
I said. Maya's nails are too long, but you can't tell a woman that.
It's like she has taken it upon herself to measure the passing of
time in a particularly rueful way. And she's wearing eye makeup,
which she's never worn before. I mean, I know our cat died a week
ago, but what has that got to do with eye makeup? "Now you're
thinking something, aren't you?" she said. "I was just thinking
about something Cameron said at work today," I said. "What did he
say?" she said. My mind went blank. I had assumed I could just
make something up on the spot, but I couldn't think of anything.
"What's for dinner?" I said. "No, I want to know what Cameron said,"
she insisted. "He said he liked ducks more than most people,"
I said. "What the heck was the context for a remark like that?" she
said. "Well, we were standing in line at the water cooler, and I
guess it was the water that made him think of ducks," I said. "And
what did you say?" she said. "Well, I wasn't going to get into an
argument with him. It was just a stupid remark," I said. "Still,
it shows you how shallow he is, how cynical. I don't want you to be
friends with him anymore, and I'm certainly not going to have him
in this house," she said. I regretted bringing Cameron into this
whole thing, especially since I hadn't even seen him that day. And
now he was banned from the house. "Cameron is one of the nicest
people I know," I said. "If you happen to be a duck," she said.
Maya had had her hair highlighted. I had just then noticed the
orange streaks against the black, like our old tabby. "I like your
hair," I said. "I had it done days ago," she said. "Yes, yes, I
know. I've been waiting for the right moment to tell you," I said.
"What's so right about this one?" she said. "The light from the
window," I said. I thought that was a rather poetic answer. "I
never know what you're thinking," she said. Then she stood up and

left the room. I don't either, I wanted to answer her, but she wouldn't believe me. So I sat there with marbles rolling around in my head. Bing, bam, bongo I could hear my watch ticking. It was running out on me. The sun was setting. "Maya, come quick, you must see this!" I shouted. "What?" she said. "It's the sunset, you must see it," I said. "I can't right now, I'm cooking," she said. I stood at the window weeping, for what I don't know. It was the most beautiful sunset I had ever seen, which probably isn't true. I just liked saying it. It sounded so dramatic. And then it was dark, and Maya called me to dinner. "So how was your day?" I said. I barely recognized her with the dark eyes and the streaked hair. Her finger-nails clicked against the table like castanets. She was apparently speaking to me, but I could barely hear anything. "Alicia . . . laundry . . . mall . . . gas. . . ." It didn't sound too bad, a normal day, like mine had been. I expected her to break into a dance, a tango maybe. Instead she said, "You know what I love about you, Warren? You have such a rich interior life. It must be like a jungle inside your head, full of exotic animals no one's ever seen before. That's why you can barely talk to me. You're too busy just keeping them all in line." "Animals with no names and nowhere to go, that's me," I said.

A Sunday Drive

We were out in the middle of nowhere when
Margot said, "Stop the car. I've got to pee."
"Jesus," I said, "where are you going to pee?"
"Behind a tree or something. It doesn't matter.
I just have to pee," she said. "Okay, but I just
hope that nobody sees you," I said, and pulled over.
I watched her walk into the woods. She was gone a
long time. I was beginning to worry, but, then, I
caught a glimpse of her, flying. The woods were
thick, and she seemed to be gliding between the
trees with the greatest of ease. I got out of
the car and walked in there for a better look.
"Margot, come down," I cried. "I can't," she yelled.
"Something bit me on the butt, and now I've got
the flying disease." I was speechless, and in awe
of her grace. It appeared so effortless and natural.
"What am I supposed to do?" I said. "I think you'd
have to put an arrow through me," she replied.
"I don't have an arrow," I said, "and besides I
could never do that. I love you!" "I think the
flying disease is for life," she said, gliding
over me. Then she was gone in a blur of light.
I walked around in circles and kicked an innocent
tree. She was being called. By who, I don't know.
But I could feel it, and it was very strong. A
Sunday drive, a pee in the woods, and now this.

Being Present at More Than One Place at a Time

I took a step and looked around. No one
was looking, so I took another step. I glanced
at the ground, looked up at the sky. Everything
seemed to be in order, so I took another step,
this one almost a hop. A woman walks up to me
and says, "That was cute." "Thanks," I say,
"watch this," and I leap high into the air.
"That's overdoing things," she says. I hang
my head, ashamed of myself. I stand there for
half an hour, not moving, barely breathing.
A cop comes up and says, "You're loitering."
"I'm not loitering," I say, "I'm repositioning
myself. I'm adjusting to the currents."
"My mistake," he says. "You had the appearance
of a loiterer." "It's the fog," I said.
When he was gone, I took a step and looked
around. I could see a vast, golden city on
the horizon. No, it's only the fog, I thought,
and jumped backward, surprising myself.

I was chasing this blue butterfly down
the road when a car came by and clipped me.
It was nothing serious, but it angered me and
I turned around and cursed the driver who didn't
even slow down to see if I was hurt. Then I
returned my attention to the butterfly which
was nowhere to be seen. One of the Doubleday
girls came running up the street with her toy
poodle toward me. I stopped her and asked,
"Have you seen a blue butterfly around here?"
"It's down near that birch tree by Grandpa's,"
she said. "Thanks," I said, and walked briskly
toward the tree. It was fluttering from flower
to flower in Mr. Doubleday's extensive garden,
a celestial blueness to soothe the weary heart.
I didn't know what I was doing there. I certain-
ly didn't want to capture it. It was like
something I had known in another life, even if
it was only in a dream, I wanted to confirm it.
I was a blind beggar on the streets of Cordoba
when I first saw it, and now, again it was here.

BOOKS BY JAMES TATE

MEMOIR OF THE HAWK
Poems

ISBN 0-06-093543-X (paperback)

"Tate's poems are meditative, introverted, self-reliant, funny, alarming, strange, difficult, intelligent, and beautifully crafted." —*New York Times Book Review*

WORSHIPFUL COMPANY OF FLETCHERS

ISBN 0-880-01431-8 (paperback)

"An impressive writer whose process of imaginative growth is through that deliberate extinction of personality which T.S. Eliot called for as the indispensable means of turning a man or woman of powerful personality into a writer of powerful poems." —*New York Times Book Review*

SHROUD OF THE GNOME

ISBN 0-880-01562-4 (paperback)

"Transforming everyday terror into sublime burlesque, Tate does his brilliant part to bolster 'the dream home under a permanent storm' against the batterings of chaos and chance."
—*Publishers Weekly* (starred review)